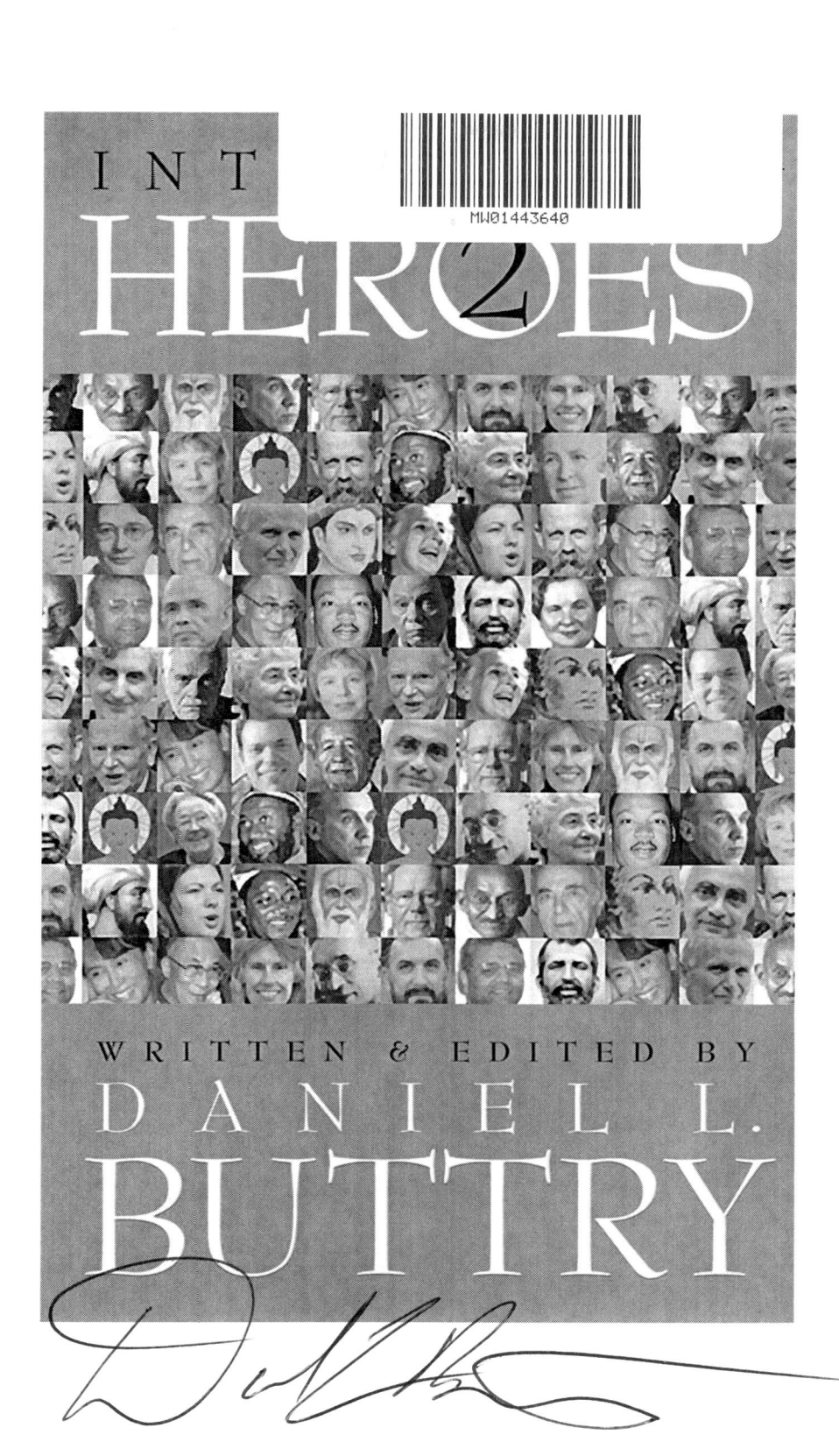

INTERFAITH HEROES 2

WRITTEN & EDITED BY
DANIEL L. BUTTRY

For ongoing discussion and additional material, visit
www.InterfaithHeroes.info

Copyright © 2009 by Daniel L. Buttry
All Rights Reserved
ISBN 978-1-934879-14-6
version 1.0

You may contact the author at
InterfaithHeroes@gmail.com

Cover art and design by
Rick Nease
www.RickNease.com

Published by
Read The Spirit Books®
an imprint of
David Crumm Media, LLC
42015 Ford Rd., Suite 234
Canton, Michigan 48187
U.S.A.

For information about customized editions, bulk purchases or permissions, contact David Crumm Media, LLC at
ReadTheSpirit@gmail.com
734-786-3815
www.ReadTheSpirit.com

Contents

Preface ix

Introduction xii

Chapter 1
Interfaith Relationships 1

Chapter 2
Pope John Paul II 6

Chapter 3
Baruch Tenembaum 10

Chapter 4
Tenzin Gyatso,
The 14th Dalai Lama 13

Chapter 5
Chiara Lubich 16

Chapter 6
Wayne Teasdale 19

Chapter 7
Ephraim Isaac 22

Chapter 8
Shanta D. Premawardhana 26

Chapter 9
David Rosen 28

Discussion Questions 31

Chapter 10
Interreligious Harmony   34

Chapter 11
Sri Ramakrishna Parmahamsa   41

Chapter 12
Hazrat Inayat Khan   44

Chapter 13
Juliet Garretson Hollister   46

Chapter 14
Hans Küng   49

Chapter 15
Joseph H. Gelberman   52

Discussion Questions   54

Chapter 16
Learning From Other Religions   56

Chapter 17
Zheng He   59

Chapter 18
Kabir   62

Chapter 19
Evelyn Underhill   65

Chapter 20
Simone Weil   67

Chapter 21
Mohandas Gandhi, Martin Luther King, Jr. and Aung San Suu Kyi   69

Chapter 22
E. Stanley Jones   75

Chapter 23
Thomas Merton   78

Chapter 24
Karen Armstrong and Bruce Feiler   82

Discussion Questions   86

Chapter 25
Religious Liberty   88

Chapter 26
Ashoka   93

Chapter 27
Abd-Ar-Rahman III and Al-Hakam II   96

Chapter 28
King John Sigismund and Isabella Jagiello   99

Chapter 29
Haym Salomon   102

Chapter 30
John Leland   105

Discussion Questions   108

Chapter 31
Providing Refuge   110

Chapter 32
Irena Sendler   115

Chapter 33
Titus Brandsma   119

Chapter 34
Si Kaddour Ben Ghabrit   122

Chapter 35
Dervis Korkut   125

Chapter 36
Corrie Ten Boom — 129

Discussion Questions — 132

Chapter 37
Building Just and Peaceful Communities — 135

Chapter 38
Charles Freer Andrews — 139

Chapter 39
Dorothy Day — 142

Chapter 40
Stephen Samuel Wise — 145

Chapter 41
Masahisa Goi — 147

Chapter 42
Richard St. Barbe Baker — 149

Chapter 43
Thich Nhat Hanh — 151

Chapter 44
Karim Al-Hussayni, Aga Khan IV — 154

Chapter 45
Sulak Sivaraksa — 157

Chapter 46
Patricia Smith Melton — 160

Chapter 47
Gaston Grandjean Dayanand — 163

Chapter 48
Ahangamage Tudor Ariyaratne — 165

Chapter 49
    Muhammed Nurayn Ashafa and James Movel Wuye   168

    Discussion Questions   172

Chapter 50
    It's Our Turn Now   175

    Sources and Credits   185

    About the Author   204

    Colophon   205

Dedication

*To my Interfaith Partners friends—I feel
like I've been surrounded by heroes*

Preface

Here's the good news: The worldwide interfaith movement is growing and deepening with each passing year. By that, first of all, I mean there is an ever-expanding interest in learning about other cultures and faiths around the world. Perhaps ironically, much of this curiosity is fueled by popular culture: music, movies, TV and especially digital culture that is now even larger than the Internet itself. For example, millions of young people now know that a red string is somehow related to the Jewish tradition of Kaballah, thanks to Madonna and other pop stars sporting red strings. These popular images we see of other faiths may be shallow or, worse yet, deeply flawed — but a healthy desire to explore world cultures is growing today.

Second, even Americans — who rank among the most religiously devout people in the world — have shed thick layers of bias toward people of other faiths and cultures. Racism and zealotry have not vanished, of course, but shoppers in their neighborhood Target stores now expect to see enormous signs for yoga gear. Although Americans continue to identify themselves as Christian in overwhelming numbers, millions now consider Eastern practices like yoga and meditation to be a natural part of daily life.

Third, we have done a terrific job of educating ourselves about tragic religious bigotry of the past. Although religious extremism still flares up in the U.S. and around the world, it's also a fact that, as a nation, we have thoroughly educated ourselves about the Holocaust, the defining religious tragedy of modern history. As recently as the 1970s, high school classrooms in the U.S. barely included references to this dark chapter in world conflict. Now, students and adults are immersed in Holocaust-related stories and educational opportunities. As a result, millions of Americans also understand the serious nature of genocides in Eastern Europe, Rwanda and Sudan as well. Sadly, we have not eliminated genocide, which often has religious roots, nor have we responded effectively in many cases to ethnic cleansing around our troubled planet. But millions of Americans now do understand the need to protect and save minorities in a way that we did not even half a century ago.

Fourth, although religious leaders around the world still have a long way to go in making peace between themselves — let alone peace between government leaders — it also is true that enormous steps have been taken by prophetic world leaders, including Pope John Paul II and so many others you will read about in this book. That is not to say that a leader like John Paul II, who balanced his interfaith inclusivity with sharp-edged enforcement of many doctrinal boundaries during his reign, should be embraced as correct in every judgment. We want you to know that many heroes you will meet in this book had flaws and limitations as well as great insights for all of humanity.

That is the major step author Dan Buttry has taken in Volume 2 of his book. This is not merely another collection of inspiring profiles, following on the 31 uplifting portraits of heroes in Volume 1. Rather, in this new book Dan explores the growth, the sophistication and the diversity of approaches unfolding around the world.

We need this kind of spiritual connection now more than ever. Forces of extremism also are hardening their pockets of "true believers" in many corners of the world — even in corners of our American homeland. No faith is immune to this problem.

While we all can celebrate larger-than-life heroes like Gandhi and Martin Luther King Jr., our turbulent times demand that all of us take first steps. As the worldwide interfaith movement expands, there are many pathways those first steps may trod.

Enjoy Volume 2 as a soul-stirring sourcebook that continues the inspiration of Volume 1 and now helps us to clarify our next steps as we continue to follow the examples of our heroes.

— *David Crumm, founding Editor of* www.ReadTheSpirit.com

Introduction

Throughout human history, people have encountered each other across religious boundaries. Sometimes those encounters have been filled with curiosity, with one or both groups exploring what they can learn from the other. Sometimes those encounters have been filled with suspicion. Those who had different ideas and rituals were viewed as a threat, and in some cases one or both groups acted with violence toward the other. Sometimes those encounters were met with bland indifference expressed in a live-and-let-live toleration.

In the 20th Century, the scientific Western World saw philosophers and even theologians proclaiming the "death of God." Religion seemed pushed to the edges of life with the spectacular growth of science and the rapid development of materialist consumer society with all its benefits. But also in that century, two world wars and the nuclear arms race showed the depths of moral depravity into which humanity could plunge and took us to the brink of extinction. In many cultures, there was an awakening of religious interest and fervor. Sometimes that passion has been expressed in extremist, exclusivist and even violent forms. But the religious ferment also has nurtured more cooperation among religious leaders than at any time in history. The shrinking of the planet through communications and travel have enabled people of diverse faiths to connect regularly, learn from each other and work together on global concerns. The 21st Century is beginning with religion as a major theme in news and other media, almost daily. Religion is shaping our politics, our international affairs and our local neighborhood relationships. Religion is haunting our dreams and spurring our hopes.

As an active participant in Interfaith Partners in Detroit (see chapter 50) I started exploring the role models in history for our interfaith cooperation. I began with the names of some people I had known—Gandhi, King, St. Francis, Roger Williams—then asked my friends in Interfaith Partners about people they knew. They referred me to King Negus, Moses Montefiore, Moussa Al-Sadr and Satguru Sivaya Subramuniyaswami—people I'd never heard of. I started putting together little biographical sketches of these folks to inspire us and guide our thinking, calling them interfaith "saints," using a Christian term, which we eventually changed to "heroes" to communicate this idea more clearly across many cultures. I stumbled across interfaith dimensions of people I knew well in other contexts, such as Howard Thurman and Fritz Eichenberg. Eventually there seemed enough for a booklet, but as I shared it with the Interfaith Partners network the response was so eager and overwhelming that people insisted that this project needed to be shared far more broadly than with just our local network. David Crumm, at that time the religion editor of the *Detroit Free Press* and coordinator of the new *ReadTheSpirit* web network offered to publish the stories as a book. Thus was born *Interfaith Heroes* in January 2008.

David suggested that we declare January as "Interfaith Heroes Month" since it coincided with both the time we were ready to release the book and also featured the national holiday for one of our main interfaith heroes, Dr. Martin Luther King, Jr. Besides publishing the book, David released one heroic story each day during January on the *ReadTheSpirit* website (www.ReadTheSpirit.com). Various friends of different religions were asked to write a response each day to the featured story. A blog was set up on *ReadTheSpirit* for readers to respond and to nominate other interfaith heroes.

We had left out a few people to make the initial book come out even with the 31 days of January. That started us thinking about a second volume. As visitors to the website submitted their nominations and I delved into research of my own, the list of additional heroes seemed to explode. There were so many people working in so many courageous and creative ways. Some were people I'd heard about but didn't know their interfaith activities. Others were people I had never known, especially those from other religious traditions. The giants in the eyes of some of my friends were people I'd never heard of, which illustrates some of the ignorance we have when we stay exclusively within the confines of our own religious communities.

So this time as I got to work on volume 2 on the Interfaith Heroes project I had a broader audience in mind as well as a more comprehensive vision for the interfaith movement around the world. Rather than merely duplicating the first volume with a string-of-pearls approach to the biographical sketches, I decided to cluster the heroes in topical sections that I'd already discerned as I was working through the earlier book. Each person seemed to have particular strengths within interfaith relationships, whether those strengths were in building relationships with people of other religions, learning from people of other traditions, providing refuge in times of danger and crisis, or working across religious lines for common concerns of justice and peace. As I gathered the heroes around each topic I realized that an opening chapter for each section would clarify each issue, help tie together the heroes of the two books, and allow the inclusion of other heroes and interfaith stories that might not work so well as a stand-alone biography. This approach also makes the adventure more compelling. Now, the two books work together on new levels. For example, if you're looking for a more detailed guide for action or further resources, turn to the first volume of *Interfaith Heroes*. We did not duplicate that in this volume.

At times in this project I found myself having to go outside my own comfort zone. I am a Christian and a passionate believer in Christ. Some of the heroes who are superb illustrations of various types of interfaith activity are also people with whom I disagree, even about the nature of interfaith relationships. We have different approaches to this work and even different concepts about the appropriate framework for such relationships. Rather than ignore such issues, I found it more helpful to note some of these issues both in the text and in the discussion questions. If we are going to build a more stable, cohesive and harmonious world coming from the diverse range of our religious traditions, then we will have to have a deeper understanding and greater honesty than has been practiced in many of our interfaith settings. We've often been acting like suitors on their first date, putting our best selves forward and avoiding the tough questions that might jeopardize the relationship in its fragile early stages. These heroes, those with whom I identify and those who are not so akin to my way of thinking, all challenge me to go deeper and to take the risks of building more real and substantial relationships with people from other faith communities. I trust that you as a reader of this book also will be stimulated and challenged to journey further with your agreements and disagreements.

Interfaith Heroes has been as interfaith community project. Many friends have suggested names, given me leads and provided research material. Others have read the manuscript and provided editorial suggestions and ideas that have enriched the final product. Special thanks go to Brenda Rosenberg, Padma Kuppa, Sheri Schiff, Bob Brutell, Eide Alawan, Victor Begg, Steve Spreitzer, Daniel Appleyard, Michael Hovey, Barbara Talley, Gail Katz, Barbara Clevinger, Ma'sood Cajee and Ken Sehested. Special thanks go to all those who nominated heroes on the website, whether the heroes ended up in chapters of this book or not. Thanks also go to three heroes with whom I was in direct contact during the writing phase: David Rosen, A.T. Ariyaratne and Shanta Premawardhana. David Crumm

Media has played a huge role in inspiring the effort, editing the manuscript and publishing and marketing the book. David and ReadTheSpirit Publisher John Hile have managed the website, passed on nominations of heroes and been a constant source of encouragement and affirmation. I especially thank my wife Sharon Buttry, an interfaith partner and leader in her own right, who has both enthusiastically and thoughtfully shared this journey and encouraged me in my writing.

In the first *Interfaith Heroes* book we thought it wise to focus just on historical figures, or as we put it in our irreverent shorthand, "dead people." But the living heroes cry out for attention, not personally but by the power of their witness and example. Some of the nominees from the website were living people, and we also discovered so many exciting things happening around the globe that needed to be pulled together in this context of identifying our interfaith heroes. I was introduced to one of the heroes in this book by one of our Interfaith Partners, Barbara Talley. Barbara directs a peace center for the Methodist district in her part of Metro Detroit, and she had sponsored an evening event with A.T. Ariyaratne from Sri Lanka during his recent tour of the United States. As "Dr. Ari" and I were chatting before the sessions, I asked him to teach me the greeting in his native Sinahala language. He said, "Ayubowan. It means: May you live long." What a delightful greeting, I thought, and perfect for me to use with this elderly man who has made such a huge impact for peace in Sri Lanka and around the world.

So we offer to all the interfaith heroes in this book who are still alive and inspire us by their work: "May you live long—Ayubowan!"

And to you — reading this page right now — may you find inspiration to become an interfaith hero yourself. And, "May you live long—Ayubowan!"

CHAPTER 1

Interfaith Relationships
"A Priest, a Minister and a Rabbi walked into…"

In the fall of 1933 the "Tolerance Trio" toured the United States. They traveled more than 9,000 miles, appearing before 129 audiences in 38 cities. The "Tolerance Trio" was not a music group introducing a new type of jazz, though they did employ an almost Vaudeville style in their rapid and often humorous interactions. They were a Protestant minister, a Catholic priest and a Jewish rabbi. This sounds like the start of a bad joke, but it was actually the start of a dynamic educational program of the newly formed National Conference of Christians and Jews (NCCJ). The trio asked each other the questions that everyone had but were afraid to say to the face of a person of the other religion: Questions about the Pope in American politics, Jewish control of the movie industry, and Protestant views on everyone else going to Hell. Together, they opened discussions between religious communities, dispelled stereotypes and gave expression to friendships that could bind people together from different religious faiths.

The National Conference of Christians and Jews (NCCJ) was established in 1927 after the Federal Council of Churches invited representatives from Jewish and Catholic groups to join in social justice and research projects. These interactions spurred further dialogue that culminated in the formation of NCCJ. NCCJ was jointly chaired by a trio drawn one each from the Jewish, Catholic and Protestant communities. Interestingly, one of the early Jewish leaders of NCCJ was Roger Williams Strauss, named after the Baptist minister who was a champion of religious liberty in founding Rhode Island and who welcomed the establishment of the second Jewish synagogue in America (Roger Williams is included in the first *Interfaith Heroes* book). NCCJ was officially renamed as the National Conference for Community and Justice in the 1990s to reflect the expanding nature of its interfaith constituency. It grew to more than 55 regional offices in 32 states working on the mission of building "whole and inclusive communities" through interfaith dialogues, anti-discrimination education and training programs for communities and workplaces, and advocacy about civil rights in areas of public policy.

NCCJ was born out of the vision and persistence of interfaith pioneers in the United States. That initial network of Jews, Catholics and Protestants had to be intentional in their efforts, because the work demanded that these already well-educated men and women explore new areas of religious scholarship. Meanwhile, they were aware of the potential for interreligious conflict. The pioneers knew that their approach across the religious boundaries might be misunderstood, misinterpreted and even deliberately distorted. In the early days of NCCJ's work, some Jews feared that the Protestants had a hidden missionary agenda, hoping to convert them. The Christians worried that the Jews were involved in interfaith activity to try to establish a new universal religion. Through deliberate intention and good will these interfaith heroes in the 1920s and 1930s fleshed out a vision of healthy interaction between the religious communities.

Building relationships with people of other faiths has been a risky venture for many years. Anti-Semitism was particularly virulent in the U.S. during the 1920s, when the Ku Klux Klan was growing nationwide, emphasizing a racist, anti-Catholic and anti-Semitic creed. The Klan ran a candidate for mayor of Detroit in 1925 who was narrowly kept out of office. The famously forged *Protocols of the Elders of Zion* trumpeted an alleged worldwide Jewish conspiracy, a document that still makes the rounds in hate groups. NCCJ and the Tolerance Trio waded into the turbulence of the social turmoil of that period with a very different message, a message of positive religious relationships and of working together as diverse religious communities to address common problems of industrialization, urbanization and international peace.

How steep are the risks? In some instances, religious conflict can help spark open warfare. Usually, conflicts are not that simplistic. In most cases, conflicts are due more to injustice, to the imbalance of political and economic power between the "haves" and the "have nots," than to particular religious issues. But, as a conflict rages, religious difference often is an easily recognizable trait, much like race, ethnicity or language, and religious affiliation becomes a short-hand way of referring to the opposing sides. Some interfaith heroes have been especially bold in forming relationships across not just lines of division, but actual battle-lines. The relationship between Francis of Assisi and Sultan Al-Malik Al-Kamil during the Crusades (featured in *Interfaith Heroes*) was a bright moment of hope in a violent chapter of human history. Though their impact on the fighting was minimal, they established a friendship and learned from each other. Today there are people of different faiths finding each other and building relationships even though the larger communities are in open war with each other.

Risks also arise within one's own religious community. Co-religionists may fear the watering down of their own religion through contact with others. They may fear losing their control over what a community defines as correct belief or correct practice. The loss of control can be political as well. In such cases, people who reach out across the lines of division can provoke strong resistance from within their particular religious community. Many interfaith heroes faced their worst attacks from within their own religious communities. Mahatma Gandhi was assassinated by a militant Hindu nationalist. Abdul Ghaffar Khan spent most of his later years in a Pakistani prison because of his vision that Muslims and Hindus could live together. Imam Moussa Al-Sadr disappeared during the Lebanese civil war not at the hand of opposing religious militias but on a peace mission to Libya. Roger Williams was banished from Massachusetts by Christians. Etty Hillesum was criticized as sounding "too Christian" by fellow Jews for talking about loving enemies. (See *Interfaith Heroes* for more on these people.) Risking the ire and even the sanction of one's own religious community is a common experience of interfaith heroes. That's one reason we call them heroes.

The primary work of some of these heroes was building these risky relationships. At the close of the 19th Century, the World's Congress of Religions was held at the World's Columbian Exposition in Chicago. Speakers at that 1893 meeting included leaders from the various streams within Christianity (Protestant, Catholic, Orthodox), Jews, Buddhists, a Muslim, a Confucian, a Zoroastrian, a Shinto and a Hindu. (Henrietta Szold, featured in *Interfaith Heroes*, was one of the Jewish speakers.)

As we enter the 21st Century there are now many networks and organizations from the local to the global level that link people of various faiths. Some of these groups are task-oriented, focused on meeting a commonly embraced human need or jointly advocating for human or civil rights. Other groups are centered on the relationships themselves, particularly on engaging in dialogue to understand and appreciate one another. Some groups provide opportunities for people from many faiths to interact; others focus on relationships between two or three faiths. In 2007, 138 Muslim scholars from 40 countries produced *A Common Word Between You and Us* to initiate dialogue between Muslim and Christian leaders for the sake of peace. Some responses from Christian leaders were very positive, while other responses from the general Christian community reflected the mistrust, animosity and misunderstanding that plague many interfaith relationships. Follow-up efforts to "A Common Word" are ongoing.

The interfaith heroes in this section all took special steps in forging relationships with people of different religions. Their overall work may have had many dimensions, but for the following heroes relationships were pivotal.

Chapter 2

Pope John Paul II
(1920-2005)

What it demands of all of us is that, holding to what we believe, we listen respectfully to one another, seek to discern all that is good and holy in each other's teachings, and cooperate in supporting everything that favors mutual understanding and peace.

The nearly 27-year papacy of John Paul II was a milestone in world history. He was greatly beloved by millions, hailed for some of his stands even beyond the membership of his own church and was criticized for other stands, surely a sign of his engagement with many of the difficult and contentious issues of the contemporary world. As the first Polish-born pope, the selection of Karol Jozef Wojtyla was a break with a long-standing tradition of electing Italian popes in the Catholic Church. His election brought fresh energy to the world-wide Catholic community, an excitement that was augmented by his frequent travels. The visit to his homeland of Poland played a role in mobilizing the opposition to Soviet Communism, which eventually brought down the Iron Curtain. But it was his teaching and symbolic actions in interreligious relationships that bring him to our attention in leading off this collection of interfaith heroes.

John Paul directly addressed the two deepest areas of religious alienation for Christians, namely the alienation of Christians with Jews and with Muslims. In addition, he took steps to heal divisions within the Christian community, between the Roman Catholic Church and the Anglican, Orthodox and Protestant churches. He backed up his action with clear statements that moved the interfaith discussions significantly forward. John Paul was the first pope to visit a synagogue (in 1986), a mosque (in 2001), and Canterbury Cathedral, seat of the Anglican Church (in 1982).

During his visit to the Synagogue in Rome, where he embraced Rabbi Toaff, John Paul repudiated interpretations of the death of Jesus that imputed collective blame on Jews as a people, past or present. He also repudiated any acts of persecution against Jews. He visited Auschwitz in 1979, praying for the dead and expressing his abhorrence for the acts of genocide committed against the Jewish people. He apologized for the silence and inaction of the Catholic Church related to the Holocaust and organized a special reflection, *We Remember: A Reflection on the Shoah,* for which he wrote the introduction calling on Catholics and Jews to work together for a world where such horror would never happen again.

As head of state at Vatican City, he recognized the State of Israel, yet also continued to recognize the plight of the Palestinian people. He lifted up a vision of Jerusalem as a meeting place of heaven and earth, a place where not only people from the three Abrahamic religions could come together, but where all people could encounter each other and encounter God in peace. In 2000, the Pope went on a pilgrimage to Israel during which he prayed at the Western Wall, inserting a written prayer for forgiveness for Christian actions against Jews in the past. Given the historical burden of hundreds of years of

Christian anti-Semitism, often sanctioned by some of this Pope's predecessors, many Jews thought John Paul did not go far enough in writings such as the *Reflection*. Nevertheless, the Anti-Defamation League said of John Paul: "More change for the better took place in his 27-year papacy than in the nearly 2,000 years before."

Though John Paul did not give as much attention to relationships between the Catholic Church and Muslims as he had with the Jewish community, there were still some historic milestones experienced in the Christian-Muslim interreligious journey through his leadership. In 2001 Pope John Paul II visited the Umayyad Mosque in Damascus, Syria, becoming the first Pope ever to visit a mosque. He said, "For all the times that Muslims and Christians have offended one another, we need to seek forgiveness from the Almighty and to offer each other forgiveness." He kissed the Quran on that trip, which brought him severe criticism from some Catholic quarters but was deeply appreciated by many of the world's Muslims.

Twice John Paul convened interfaith prayer services for peace in Assisi. He was a special friend of the Dalai Lama, as they shared together their burdens of religious repression from Communist governments and desires for world peace. He issued many statements of apology and asked forgiveness for actions taken throughout history by various leaders of the Catholic Church. Sometimes he was joined by others in mutual expressions of openness. Sometimes he was met with suspicion or demands to do more. Whatever the response to his actions, he sought to heal many long-standing rifts caused by religion, especially by his own Roman Catholic Church. Pope John Paul II took steps that few others in his position have been willing to take.

In his address to Jewish, Muslim and Christian leaders in Jerusalem in 2000, John Paul said: "The Catholic Church wishes to pursue a sincere and fruitful interreligious dialogue with the members of the Jewish faith and followers of Islam. Such a dialogue is not an attempt to impose our views upon others.

What it demands of all of us is that, holding to what we believe, we listen respectfully to one another, seek to discern all that is good and holy in each other's teachings, and cooperate in supporting everything that favors mutual understanding and peace."

This charge can help all of us to build stronger interfaith relationships with respect and spiritual integrity.

Chapter 3

Baruch Tenembaum
(b. 1933)

The agreement is based on respect, the knowledge and understanding of our rights that each one of us can be different from the other.

Baruch Tenembaum was born in Sante Fe, Argentina, a settlement for Jewish immigrants fleeing the violence of Russian pogroms in the late 19th Century. A son of Jewish-Argentine cowboys—*gauchos*—he entered academia, teaching the Hebrew and Yiddish languages, Yiddish literature, the Hebrew Scriptures and philosophy. He also became a businessman, establishing the Israeli Tourist Office in Buenos Aires.

A central passion to Tenembaum's life has been Jewish-Christian relationships, particularly relationships between Jews and the Catholic Church. He used his position as a travel agent to organize a group of Argentine Catholic priests to visit the Holy Land. Out of that trip, working with his friends among Catholic clergy and other businesspeople, Tenembaum helped establish the *Casa Argentina en Jerusalem* which hosted opportunities for Catholics and Jews to get together and learn from each other. Tenembaum then decided to move from working with the priests to inviting the pope to visit Israel. During a visit to the Vatican in 1965, Tanembaum personally invited Pope Paul VI to visit Jerusalem, which resulted in the first such visit to that holy city by a pope.

Tenembaum promoted the idea of establishing interfaith monuments. His first major project was the commissioning of a fresco by the Argentine painter Raul Soldi in the main church in Nazareth, which was finished in 1968 and has been seen by more than 10 million people. He also organized the production of a memorial mural dedicated to victims of the Holocaust in the Buenos Aires Cathedral. In April 1997 the mural, containing Jewish religious texts, was unveiled by the Cardinal of Argentina, Antonio Quarracino, Polish Nobel Peace Prize winner Lech Walesa and Tenembaum. A replica of the mural was made in the Vatenrunser Church in Berlin.

Tenembaum's interfaith work ended up putting his life at risk. A terrorist group associated with the Argentine military dictatorship kidnapped him in 1976. They accused him of "infecting the Catholic Church with the virus of Judaism" and "of spreading ideas of alleged coexistence so as to destroy Christian principles." When his wife Perla volunteered to be a hostage, she was kidnapped as well. Eventually they were released in large part due to the mediation and advocacy efforts of a Catholic priest, Father Horacio Moreno.

Following the kidnapping, Tenembaum left Argentina for the U.S. He sought out Gentiles who had helped Jews during the Holocaust. With the help of Congressman Tom Lantos, a Holocaust survivor, he founded The International Raoul Wallenberg Foundation to promote the life and work of Raoul Wallenberg. Wallenberg was a Swedish diplomat stationed in Hungary who saved almost 100,000 Jews from deportation to the death camps. Wallenberg was seized by the Soviet Army at the end of the war, and he was never seen again. Tenembaum established the Wallenberg Foundation to fight intolerance, racism and violence and to stimulate the courage to defend the weak against aggression and violence. More than 60 heads of state and 30 Nobel Prize laureates are members of the Wallenberg Foundation. One of the stories highlighted by the foundation is that of Irena Sendler (see Chapter 32).

Tenembaum has continued to work on issues of interfaith dialogue and reconciliation. He sees fear as the fuel that touches off crimes of religious violence. Getting to know someone enables people to let go of their fears, about which Tenembaum said, "This simple and basic principle is the main base of the interconfessional dialogue." His perspective on interfaith dialogue and relationships was not to find the lowest common denominator between faiths or to simply tolerate people who were different. He said, "The agreement is not about faith or theological beliefs. Each of us will continue sticking to his or her faith, and his or her source of inspiration. The agreement is based on respect, the knowledge and understanding of our rights that each one of us can be different from the other."

CHAPTER 4

Tenzin Gyatso, The 14th Dalai Lama
(b. 1935)

Each religion has certain unique ideas or techniques, and learning about them can only enrich one's own faith.

Tenzin Gyatso was born in a rural village in Tibet. Following the practices of Tibetan Buddhism he was recognized as the 14th reincarnation of the Dalai Lama. Dalai Lamas are believed to be the manifestation of Avalokiteshvara (also known as Chenrezig), the Bodhisattva or "enlightened being" of compassion and the patron saint of Tibet.

As the Dalai Lama, Tenzin Gyatso began his monastic education at the age of 6. He received his doctorate in Buddhist philosophy at 23, but prior to completing his education, politics intervened to shape his life in a dramatic fashion.

In October, 1950, China invaded Tibet, and the next month the Dalai Lama assumed full political power in the Tibetan government where the Dalai Lama has traditionally been the absolute ruler. He initially sought to work within the Chinese Communist system. Then in 1959 there was a failed uprising by Tibetans that prompted the Dalai Lama to flee to India and set up a government in exile. Tens of thousands of Tibetans followed him into exile, leaving Tibet for India and other parts of the world.

In exile the Dalai Lama began a thorough overhaul of the Tibetan political system. He abandoned the traditional heavy-handed feudalistic system and established democratic reforms in both the government-in-exile and in the plans for a constitution for a free Tibet. He sought nonviolent means for liberating Tibet, offering a peace proposal including negotiations with China. Those efforts were recognized with the awarding of the Nobel Peace Prize in 1989. In 2008 in the lead-up to the Beijing Olympics, another uprising and violent repression in Tibet focused world attention on the situation in that mountainous region. Shortly after the crisis initial contacts were made between the Dalai Lama and the Chinese government to open new negotiations to resolve the status of Tibet, though once again Tibetan hopes and dreams were frustrated when the talks failed to achieve any political change.

His political efforts might seem enough to consume a lifetime, but the Dalai Lama has also emerged as a leader in global interfaith efforts. In articulating his three major commitments, his first is the promotion of human values such as compassion, forgiveness, tolerance, contentment and self-discipline. His second is to harmony and understanding among the world's religious traditions. The third commitment is to the people of Tibet as their Dalai Lama. In pursuit of religious harmony he has met repeatedly with other global religious figures such as the Catholic Popes Paul VI and John Paul II and the Chief Rabbi of Israel as well as senior Muslim, Hindu, Sikh and Eastern Orthodox leaders. He sees the exchange of ideas and feelings between leaders of different religions as a way to "open the door to a progressive pacification between people."

The Dalai Lama is more than the formal head of a major religious group appearing in global religious congresses. He has gotten directly involved in the organizing and planning of such events. This direct involvement in interreligious affairs and events has led to many deep interpersonal relationships with people of other faiths. Those close to him have testified about his impact in their lives. Working with other contemplatives of different religions in the Monastic Interreligious Dialogue, the Dalai Lama helped produce the *Universal Declaration on Nonviolence*. At the World Congress of Faith he said, "Each religion has certain unique ideas or techniques, and learning about them can only enrich one's own faith." Through his relationships with so many religious leaders the Dalai Lama may have enriched his own faith, but countless people of other religions bear witness about how he has enriched their faith, as well.

CHAPTER 5

Chiara Lubich
(1920-2008)

During World War II on the night of May 13, 1944, Allied bombers devastated the city of Trent. Many residents fled to the surrounding mountains, but one woman, Chiara Lubich, whose home was destroyed, had a life-changing religious experience. She met a woman in the ruins who had lost all four of her children and was crazy with grief. As Chiara tried to comfort the mother, she felt she was being asked to embrace the suffering of humanity. Her experience had roots months earlier when in a small chapel she was overwhelmed by God's love and changed her name from Silvia to Chiara in honor of the woman saint who worked with Francis of Assisi ("Clare" in English).

After the war she met Igino Giordani, a journalist and member of the Italian Parliament, and Pasquale Foresi, who eventually became a Catholic priest. Together they launched Focolare, a movement that has grown to well over 100,000 members in 182 nations. The vision of Focolare, which means "hearth" or "family fireside," was rooted in Jesus' prayer in the Gospel of John, chapter 17, "That they may all be one." Lubich sought to "bring an invasion of love in the world." Through the power of spirituality she specifically addressed some of the long-standing prejudices and conflicts that divide humanity.

Though the Focolare movement is rooted in the Roman Catholic tradition, it includes Christians from other traditions (Protestant, Anglican and Orthodox) and people of other religions (Jewish, Muslim, Hindu, Buddhist, Sikh and Baha'i) as well as people who claim no particular religion. They seek to foster dialogues across Christian confessional lines, across religious lines and across political lines. Lubich hosted many sessions of political dialogue in which she challenged national leaders to "love the nation of the other as you love your own." Within the Christian community she called for improved ecumenical relations and worked toward communion among the different traditions of Christianity. She encouraged believers of different religions to affirm and foster together universal values that respect our common humanity. Even people of no religious affiliation could join in supporting values such as freedom, respect for human rights, solidarity and peace.

Lubich's encouragement of dialogue resulted in doors being opened for her to speak in places Christian lay women were not known to frequent, such as before 800 Buddhist monks and nuns in Thailand, with 3,000 African-American Muslims at the Malcolm Shabazz Mosque in Harlem, New York, and before the Jewish community in Buenos Aires. She received recognition from UNESCO and the Council of Europe and many other political and religious bodies for her peace education and defense of individual and social rights.

Some people have criticized the intensity and rigorousness that a commitment to life within the Focolare movement required. Other critics have attacked conservative moral stances by Focolare, and yet others have made accusations of syncretism and have charged that Focolare is trying to develop one world faith. Through all this criticism, however, Lubich remained within the Roman Catholic Church and expressed her spirituality within the terms of the Christian Scriptures. To those outside the movement she was respected for fostering dialogue across class, generation, political and ethnic lines as well as religious lines. She was clear in explaining that her passion for crossing religious boundaries arose within her own religious faith. She didn't require that others share her same religious source. Instead, she encouraged people to meet to work together on shared problems. By living out that message Lubich became an inspiration for people of many faiths.

Chapter 6

Wayne Teasdale
(1945-2004)

If the two traditions work together on resolving critical issues facing the planet, and if they commit themselves to an open-ended dialogue process in which mutual influence on each other occurs in the areas of belief or view, prayer, and social engagement, they will make an enormously precious contribution towards the communication of a new consciousness all around the world.

Wayne Teasdale's spiritual career began as a Trappist monk at St. Joseph's Abbey in Massachusetts. After 10 years under the direction of Abbott Thomas Keating, founder of the centering prayer movement, Teasdale received an invitation that changed the direction of his spiritual journey. He was invited to study in India at the Benedictine ashram of Bede Griffiths. Griffiths was a proponent of dialogue between the Hindu and Catholic religions and had incorporated many Hindu spiritual practices into his Christian mysticism. Teasdale learned much from Griffiths and underwent a ritual of sanyassa in which one "renounces the world." In this understanding of spirituality, "renunciation" means a selfless embrace of the world in religious faith.

Interreligious dialogue became a central passion in Teasdale's work. He especially felt drawn to Buddhism and developing a mutually beneficial learning experience between the contemplative traditions of Buddhism and Christianity. He said, "I am convinced that Christianity and Buddhism together have a unique opportunity and responsibility to enter into a sustained dialogue on all matters. If the two traditions work together on resolving critical issues facing the planet, and if they commit themselves to an open-ended dialogue process in which mutual influence on each other occurs in the areas of belief or view, prayer, and social engagement, they will make an enormously precious contribution towards the communication of a new consciousness all around the world."

Teasdale developed a relationship with the Dalai Lama, and together they served on the board of trustees for the Council for a Parliament of the World's Religions. They helped convene the 1993 Parliament of the World's Religions that 8,000 people attended in Chicago (See Chapter 14). Teasdale also was co-director for the Synthesis Dialogues, a forum that the Dalai Lama moderated that brought together people from many spiritual traditions and professional disciplines to explore ways to expand human awareness.

As Teasdale engaged in these relationships, especially crossing to connect with Hindu and Buddhist traditions, he developed an understanding he termed "interspirituality." With that term, he referred to a perspective in which one sees a degree of commonality in the world's religions that can be approached through mystical experience. He was a part of the Monastic Interreligious Dialogue, a network of Catholic Benedictine and Trappist monks and nuns who sought to engage the monastic and contemplative traditions of other religions for mutual learning. Representing the Monastic Interreligious Dialogue, Teasdale worked with Thomas Keating, the Dalai Lama and others to produce the *Universal Declaration on Nonviolence*, built upon the ideals Gandhi established in his teaching on *satyagraha* (see *Interfaith Heroes*, Chapter 12).

In his renunciation of the world for his own sake, he gave himself to the world for the world's sake, engaging in many social issues. Inspired by his relationship with the Dalai Lama, he became a leader in the Interfaith Call for Freedom of Worship and Human Rights in Tibet. For Teasdale, interfaith relationships enabled him to go deeper into the Spirit of God and at the same time to go deeper into the struggles in the world.

CHAPTER 7

Ephraim Isaac

Understanding spiritual and cultural matters in perspective, we can acquire wisdom which helps us to live with our fellow human beings in peace—knowing our limitations, respecting others, appreciating non-material things.

Ethiopia is a country of religious diversity that sometimes has been famed for its tolerance (see the story of King Negus providing refuge to the disciples of Muhammad in Interfaith Heroes, Chapter 1). In recent years, however, Ethiopia has known much political turmoil with ethnic and religious conflict interwoven in political disputes. Orthodox Christians make up about 50% of the population and Muslims about 33%. Yet an Ethiopian Jewish scholar has become the leading voice and activist for peace.

Ephraim Isaac is from the tiny Yemenite Jewish community in Ethiopia that had been isolated from Western Judaism until the 19th Century. (Yemenite Jews are not necessarily from the country of Yemen, but are adherents of a particular branch of Judaism that traces itself to

Late Second Temple expressions of the Jewish faith.) While retaining his Ethiopian citizenship and residence, Isaac was hired as the first professor of Afro-American Studies at Harvard University. He lectured and wrote in the areas of African languages, ancient religions, black civilizations and slavery. He has been a very popular teacher and a widely sought-after lecturer at prominent academic institutions around the world. But he also has been concerned for those at the bottom levels of education. He co-founded the National Literacy Campaign Organization, which taught 1.5 million Ethiopians to read. After years in academia and in efforts to address national issues, such as literacy, Isaac became a respected "elder" among Ethiopians.

During the civil wars that devastated so much of Ethiopia in the late 1980s and early 1990s Ephraim Isaac sought to employ Ethiopian cultural traditions of using elders to mediate between the government and armed opposition groups. As a mediator, Isaac spoke about the Ethiopian tradition of shimagele-jarsa in which the mediating elder exercises sympathetic listening, respect for each side, patience, broadmindedness, impartiality and advocacy for serious dialogue. He organized people recognized as elders to help political leaders try to find the way to sustainable peace agreements. These elders were eventually constituted as the Peace and Development Committee (PDC) with Isaac as the Chair. The PDC brought together religious leaders from the Christian, Muslim and Jewish communities and from various social and professional sectors of society to work on reconciliation issues following the collapse of the Marxist Derg regime in 1992. The PDC has continued to mediate amid the social and political conflicts in Ethiopia.

Ephraim Isaac participated in the Parliament of World Religions held in 1993, 1999 and 2004. He affirmed the crucial need to foster interreligious dialogue and cooperation to address the challenging issues before humanity. He especially focused his work on the reduction of violence that was either motivated by religion or which targeted people because of their religion. He was one of the original signatories of the

"Declaration towards a Global Ethic" (see Chapter 14 on Hans Kung), which sought peace among religions built upon dialogue and investigation of the common foundations of religion. The representatives committed themselves to build cultures of nonviolence, solidarity, tolerance and equal rights for men and women.

Ephraim Isaac did not just participate in making grand statements, but labored within the conflicts of Ethiopia to bring those grand ideals to fruition. He spoke about religious tolerance, organized elders to work for peace, and even became an interreligious peacemaker. As Ethiopia went through tumultuous times following the civil war, he organized an Interfaith Prayer Day, held on the Ethiopian New Year. The service was opened by the head of the Ethiopian Orthodox Church. A Muslim imam led in prayer and gave a sermon, as did the Catholic cardinal and the head of the Protestant churches in Ethiopia. Finally Isaac, representing the Jewish community, spoke on the need for peace, reconciliation and courage to overcome the past.

Isaac continued his religious peacemaking in many spheres. He organized a conference in Yemen to help Muslims and Jews improve their relationships. When a dispute erupted between archbishops of the Ethiopian Orthodox Church, this Jewish elder helped the Christian leaders settle their dispute. Isaac was invited into this mediating role because he had established relationships with high-ranking church officials through his years in academia specializing in studies of the Geez language used by the Church. Isaac even traveled to Northern Ireland to assist in the peace process there between Catholics and Protestants.

His Jewish faith, especially drawing upon the writings of the prophets Isaiah and Jeremiah, gave powerful inspiration and guidance to Isaac in his peacemaking efforts. He could also quote the Christian New Testament from 1 John about loving one's brother. "Peace and love are related," he said, "Love and respect are related." In an amazing demonstration of interfaith respect to a Christian musical masterpiece, Isaac translated Handel's *Messiah* into Amharic, the main language of Ethiopia. Then in a speech about the way to peace and reconciliation, Isaac said, "Understanding spiritual and cultural matters in perspective, we can acquire wisdom which helps us to live with our fellow human beings in peace—knowing our limitations, respecting others, appreciating non-material things."

CHAPTER 8

Shanta D. Premawardhana
(b. 1952)

Shanta D. Premawardhana is the Director of Interreligious Dialogue and Cooperation for the World Council of Churches in Geneva, Switzerland. He came to that position by providing leadership in interfaith relationships from the local to the national and finally to the global level. Interfaith relations have been a passion throughout his life.

Born in Sri Lanka into a Christian family, Premawardhana was raised in an ecumenical and interreligious milieu. After his seminary training in Sri Lanka and India, he came to the United States for further graduate studies in the area of comparative religions. He founded the Chicago Ashram of Jesus Christ in Skokie, Illinois to reach out to South Asian immigrants. One of his programs involved small interfaith dialogue groups in which people of various religious traditions would come together in each other's homes and share about their differing faith journeys and learn from each other.

Later as pastor of the Ellis Avenue Church, a Baptist church in Chicago, he became president of one of the oldest interfaith organizations in the U.S., the Hyde Park and Kenwood Interfaith

Council, founded in 1911. In his leadership capacity of this organization of Christians, Hindus, Muslims and Jews, he trained people in interfaith dialogue. Within his own Christian community he offered courses in "Removing Anti-Judaism from the Pulpit." He also was involved in the Gamaliel Foundation, an interfaith network that engaged in issues of community organizing for economic justice and immigrant rights.

His interfaith leadership in Chicago brought Premawardhana to the attention of the National Council of Churches USA (NCC). The NCC called him to direct their Interfaith Relations Commission. From 2003 to 2007 he coordinated the interfaith activities of the NCC and their member denominations. One major initiative was the interfaith fast for an end to the war in Iraq, which Premawardhana helped organize. From dawn to dusk interfaith gatherings were held in the United States as well as in Canada and Australia. The fast was broken at Islamic centers with an *iftar* dinner on the "Night of Power," the holiest night in Ramadan, the Muslim month of fasting. Following the dinner at the Islamic Center in Sterling, Virginia, Premawardhana challenged the Muslims, Jews and Christians gathered together to expand and deepen the interfaith relationships they had made through their shared concern for peace.

Premawardhana says, "Interreligious relations are a critical need in today's world." He sees the U.S. experience in this regard as unusual, compared with most of the world, because people in the U.S. can engage in discussions with those of other religions on the basis of their religious convictions alone. But in most of the world "faith cannot be separated from culture, politics, nationality, in other words, identity. So it is more complex. That complexity is exciting to me." Interfaith relationships then become a critical point for dealing with the entire web of human relationships, touching all the various aspects of our conflicts and hopes for community.

Chapter 9

David Rosen

(b. 1951)

According to our faith traditions, killing innocents in the name of God is a desecration of His Holy Name, and defames religion in the world.

The breadth of Rabbi David Rosen's life and work spans the globe from South to North and from the center of Judaism to the center of Catholicism. He was born in 1951 in England, the son of a prominent rabbi. After an education in England and Jerusalem he went to Israel where he served in the Israeli Defense Forces as a chaplain.

Rosen then went to South Africa where he became Senior Rabbi to the largest Jewish congregation in the country. In that context his interfaith work began. He was the founder and chairman of the Cape Inter-Faith Forum, a council of Jews, Christians and Muslims working on interfaith dialogue and issues in the South African context. From there he was appointed as Chief Rabbi of Ireland, in which capacity he was a co-founder of the Irish Council of Christians and Jews.

He returned to Israel in 1985 to enter academia, eventually becoming Professor of Jewish Studies at the Jerusalem Center for Near Eastern Studies. From his base in Jerusalem he became a leading figure in interfaith dialogue, taking leadership in many organizations that dealt with interreligious issues. He became the face of Judaism to much of the interfaith movement, chairing the International Jewish Committee on Interreligious Consultations and directing the American Jewish Committee's Department for Interreligious Affairs and Heilbrunn Institute for International Interreligious Understanding. He participated in the World Economic Forum's "C-100" event, a gathering of 100 world leaders seeking to improve relationships between Muslims and non-Muslims.

Rabbi Rosen became the first Israeli citizen and the first Orthodox Rabbi to be made a Knight Commander of the Order of Gregory the Great, a Roman Catholic honor bestowed upon Rabbi Rosen by Pope Benedict XVI in 2005. This groundbreaking honor was given to acknowledge the contribution Rabbi Rosen has made to Jewish-Catholic reconciliation. He played a pivotal role in the negotiations between Israel and the Vatican that led to establishing full diplomatic relationships between these two nations so deeply intertwined with religious leadership and their global communities. Earlier, at the invitation of Pope John Paul II, Rabbi Rosen participated in the World Day of Prayer for Peace convened in Assisi, Italy.

In 1988, Rabbis for Human Rights was formed in Israel to be a rabbinic voice of conscience. Rabbi Rosen played a leading role in forming this organization in the tradition of the Hebrew prophets. The organization included Reform, Orthodox, Conservative, Reconstructionist and Renewal rabbis and students. The Rabbis for Human Rights advocated for the causes of the poor, including the rights of Israel's minorities, Palestinians, Bedouins, Ethiopian Jews, women, and others in need of a voice for their concerns. They specifically engaged in interfaith work, creating dialogue and joint projects with Christian, Muslim, Druze and other Jewish leaders.

In 2002, the Middle East Interfaith Summit was held in Alexandria, Egypt with Muslim, Christian and Jewish religious leaders from the Holy Land. The statement from conference leaders affirmed: "According to our faith traditions, killing innocents in the name of God is a desecration of His Holy Name, and defames religion in the world. The violence in the Holy Land is an evil which must be opposed by all people of good faith. We seek to live together as neighbors respecting the integrity of each other's historical and religious inheritance."

A similar meeting was held in 2006 at the 8th Assembly of the World Conference of Religions for Peace, for which Rabbi Rosen is the President. Religions for Peace includes people from more than 100 countries and many different religions. Working alongside moderator Prince El Hassan bin Talal of Jordan to tackle issues of violence with religious dimensions, Rabbi Rosen addressed the thorny issue of identity in conflicts. "Every leader is going to find justification for the position of the community he or she is part of since religion seeks to give meaning to who we are, which is bound up with our identities. So when our identities are threatened we seek to defend them." Out of the pain of conflict, people will cling to their religious identities for a sense of purpose and self-justification, which also can stigmatize "the other" in the conflict. Rosen spoke about how politicians, as they work on peace-building, usually try to keep away from religion because religion is so intimately tied up with identity. But Rosen called for a deeper constructive partnership between political and religious leaders in finding the ways to peace, especially in the Holy Land. For Rosen, that very religious identity that causes so many problems can also be the key in finding a basis and motivation for building a genuine peace. In those religious identities and teachings are the roots for our dreams of peace, our values of human rights and our standards of justice.

❓ Discussion Questions
Chapters 1-9

Commonality vs. Difference: This is one of the key issues that arises as one engages in interfaith dialogue. How do we understand — and negotiate within our own lives — the boundaries between our faith and other faiths?

On the one hand there can be a concern that too close a connection (such as the "interspiritual" view offered by Wayne Teasdale) compromises basic elements of one's own religion (in Teasdale's case as a Christian, perhaps the place of the Bible and the uniqueness of Jesus Christ). On the other hand there can be such an exclusivist view of the truth of one's own religion, or perhaps the spiritual superiority of one's religion as the last legitimate divine revelation, that genuine relationships of mutual respect are impossible to build. Some religions explicitly embrace the fundamental unity of all religions, whereas other religions have some dimensions of exclusivity or precedence for their religion in relation to others. How can we establish authentic relationships with people who are religiously different and, at the same time, maintain our own faithful integrity?

What insights do you draw from famous examples? John Paul II and Baruch Tenembaum articulated their understandings of the relationships we could have as we engage in interfaith dialogue. Both wanted to maintain strong understandings of their own faiths even as they listened and learned from others. How do you assess their approaches to dialogue?

In the guide for "Monastic Interreligious Dialogue," it was suggested that the ideal personal requirements for a Christian monk to engage in interfaith dialogue should include: being firmly rooted and centered in the Christian tradition, being personally mature, being eager for a deep knowledge of other religions and ready to rethink the ways given to express the Christian faith, being open to strangers and persons of different backgrounds and status, and being attentive to the infinite ways in which the Holy Spirit is made manifest. What do you think of these requirements?

If you are not a Christian, what requirements would you suggest for a person to prepare to engage in interfaith dialogue? Rabbi David Rosen says it is necessary to seek "to understand the other the way the other understands him or herself." What challenges does that pose to you? How might you best develop that understanding?

When Ephraim Isaac was a child, the Italians invaded Ethiopia. For two days, he sheltered in a bunker under a constant bombardment from the Italians. When the explosions ceased, he emerged to find that his best friend had been killed. This tragedy helped shape his passion for peacemaking. Chiara Lubich developed a similar motivation for peace as a young woman surviving the Allied bombing of her city in Italy during World War II. How have your experiences early in life shaped your interest for knowing people who are different? Or, have experiences early in your life raised anxieties about people from different faiths or ethnicities?

Ephraim Isaac called for being honest about oneself and one's religion if reconciliation is to be genuine. He said, "Religious peace comes through respecting both self and tradition—A prayer meeting where a Christian does not say the name of Jesus is not honest; it is a show. To live together, we must remain honest and true to our respective faiths and respect one another." Do you agree or disagree with this, and why? Can we pray with people of other faiths in ways that show our own beliefs yet also not offend others? Or to put the shoe on the other foot, can we hear another pray in ways that might be radically different for us and not take offense? How do we hear and receive the heart of another person when we pray from different traditions?

Chapter 10

Interreligious Harmony

Encountering the Good and the Holy in One Another

Religious harmony? You have got to be kidding! Just look at history. Violence against idol worshipers in ancient Israel. War over leadership succession that lead to the split between Sunni and Shi'a Muslims. Pogroms against Jews in Christian Europe. The Crusades with Western Christians fighting Muslims for control of the "Holy Land" as well as fighting Orthodox Christians along the way. People being tortured in the Inquisition at the hands of the Christian Catholic Church hierarchy. Religious wars in Europe lasting one hundred years pitting Protestant Reformers against Catholics in varying configurations. The conquest of the Americas with the cross and the sword. Violence against Mormons in 19th Century U.S.

Just look at the news over the last few years. Muslim extremists flying planes into buildings to attack "infidels." Hindu militants killing Muslims in Gujarat and burning churches in Orissa, India. Protestants fighting Catholics in Northern Ireland. Christians fighting Muslims, Muslims fighting other Muslims, Christians fighting other Christians, everyone fighting Druze and Alawites in the civil war in Lebanon. A Jewish extremist settler in the West Bank shooting worshipers in a mosque. Muslims and Christians battling in the streets of Nigeria, burning churches and mosques. Hindus and Sikhs battling over the Golden Temple in Amristar. The Taliban blowing up ancient Buddhist statues in Afghanistan. Muslim militants going down in a violent siege of a mosque in Pakistan. Mosques being destroyed in sectarian violence in the midst of the war in Iraq. Christians, Bahá'ís, Yazidis, Zoroastrians, and Mandaeans driven out of Iran and Iraq by militant expressions of Islam.

This prevalence of religious disharmony and violence makes us think of the plaintive plea of Rodney King during the 1992 riot (or uprising) in Los Angeles: "Can we all get along?" All the religions claim to teach values of love, peace and justice, yet the violence seems to go on and on.

Today's assertive atheists like to claim that religion inevitably leads to violence. To be honest, however, some of the worst atrocities in human history have been perpetrated under atheistic ideologies. Communism under Stalin, Mao, and Pol Pot produced the slaughter of tens of millions of people. Nazism under Hitler (albeit with the quietistic complicity of many Lutherans and Catholics) carried out the Holocaust in which 6 million Jews perished along with many others deemed "unworthy" to live. Perhaps the issue isn't so much religious as human. Almost all the religious conflicts involve issues of political or economic power at the core, over which religion is sometimes used as a convenient form of justification or inspiration to militancy.

Yet all these faiths have teachings and traditions that speak of love, generosity, unity, mercy, and building just and peaceful communities. Throughout this same history and even in the middle of some of these experiences of violence there can be co-religionists who demonstrate commitments to coexistence or even to building unity across the differences. The seeds of religious harmony are present in all the traditions, whether or not they are allowed to germinate, grow and bear fruit in any particular social and political context.

What is the basis for religious harmony? The answer to that question has been varied even within the interfaith movement.

One answer is that all religions are basically one. According to this approach there is a basic unity of the divine that is expressed in particular religions. All those religions have equally valid truths, being reflections on the one deeper truth behind them all.

This is the view that characterizes many expressions of Hinduism. The Swami Vivekananda, a disciple of Sri Ramakrishna (see Chapter 10), during a tour in North America, including an appearance before the World's Parliament of Religions in 1893, spoke about the divine as the great big ocean. Each religion is like a frog in a well. "I am a Hindu. I am sitting in my own little well and thinking that the whole world is my little well. The Christians sit in their little well and think the whole world is their well. The Muslims sit in their little well and think that is the whole world." God is bigger than any one faith can grasp. All faiths have their place and value. Vivekananda quoted a Hindu hymn from his childhood: "As the different streams having their sources in different places all mingle their water in the sea, so, O Lord, the different paths which people take through different tendencies, various though they appear, crooked or straight, all lead to Thee." Within this context religions should relate to each other not through conversion from one to the other, but through learning from each other with respect from within one's own tradition. As he told the Parliament of Religions: "The Christian is not to become a Hindu or a Buddhist, nor a Hindu or a Buddhist to become a Christian. But each must assimilate the spirit of the others and yet preserve their individuality and grow according to their own law of growth."

Swami Vivekananda

The Baháʼí faith has made the unity of all religions one of its basic tenets. ʻAbdu'l-Bahá is included among the fundamental doctrines of the Baháʼí faith: "the basic unity of all religions;

the condemnation of all forms of prejudice, whether religious, racial, class or national." He taught oneness among all humanity; religion was to be for the protection of all peoples and nations. Bahá'ís believe that all religions come from the same source, the one God. Each person should hold fast to the faith that draws them. But as our world grows closer together we need each religious tradition to strive for that deeper understanding and unity rooted in the very nature of God. Thus interfaith work and striving for harmony is perhaps the key challenge of the age within the Bahá'í framework.

Similar teachings appear in other traditions. With varying viewpoints and emphases these traditions find their way to religious harmony by embracing one particular religious belief or tradition, but seeing it as one among many valid religious paths. The Indian-American Sikh writer, Bhagat S. Thind, expressed this perspective in his writings: "There are many religions, but only one Morality, one Truth, and one God. The only Heaven is one of conscious life and fellowship with God." Springing out of Western Christianity in the 18th and 19th Century, there were New Thought movements, the Unitarian Universalism and Unity. Though sounding similar, Unitarianism and Unity gave different views of religious harmony. Unitarianism grew up in a variety of manifestations and versions in the U.S. in the 18th Century. Unitarianism in its beginning was strictly monotheistic and anti-Trinitarian, thus seeing itself in contrast to the traditional Catholic, Orthodox and Protestant expressions of Christianity. Early Unitarians generally embraced the core ethical teachings of Jesus, seeing him as a prophet, but not as divine. They held reason in spirituality as very important. The Unitarians valued the religious teachings of other traditions even though most saw the teachings of Jesus and the Bible as central to their own spiritual expression. In the late 1800s and into the early 1900s Charles Fillmore established Unity through a merging of his views on science and the teachings of Jesus. He sought a daily practical application of the truths in Jesus' teachings. He believed God's spirit is within all people, and that all people are inherently good. Therefore, there should be no discrimination against people of other religions, for all people can have spiritual understanding. The challenge from the viewpoint of Unity is to actually live by that spiritual understanding.

Other religions and traditions are more exclusive in their beliefs, especially Judaism, Christianity and Islam, which all believe strongly in an individual revelation of God, creating special communities of faith such as the covenant people Israel, or the Church as the Body of Christ, or the Muslim *umah* or community of faith. In particular, Christianity and Islam are known as missionary religions, spreading their faith to others and seeking conversion. Buddhism also has been a missionary faith spread by traveling teachers, even though the core of the religion does not include a belief in a divine being. Basic Buddhism is rather a belief in a philosophy embodied in the "Four Noble Truths" and a set of spiritual practices set forth in the "Noble Eightfold Path." Christianity, Islam and even the universalist Bahá'í faith also believe in "supercession," that their key revealer of the faith, whether Jesus, Muhammad or Bahá'u'lláh, was the ultimate or final prophet bringing God's revelation. So how can such faiths engage in harmonious religious relationships? Must they give up core beliefs that would essentially be a renunciation of their faith?

For these faiths religious harmony is not found in saying that "we all believe in the same God," or that "what matters is that one is sincere." For these faiths harmony is not established on the basis of believing there is one Truth behind all the particular religious expressions. Rather the basis is found in human relationships of respect and humility. Even though we hold our beliefs very deeply, we can recognize that even with our disagreements there is still much we can learn from each other. Furthermore, we can cooperate with each other in building better societies, for so much of our ethical teaching follows similar values, built upon core beliefs of love, justice and peace. As Pope John Paul II said, speaking of interfaith dialogue, "What it demands of all of us is that, holding to what we believe, we listen respectfully to one another, seek to discern all that is good and holy in each other's teachings, and cooperate in supporting everything that favors mutual understanding and peace."

Some will come at the issue of interreligious relationships and harmony by immediately focusing on the nature of God. They will see this as the doorway toward cooperation. But not all religious groups will find this the most helpful doorway. Others will move toward interreligious relationships by focusing on the nature of humanity. They will find it more helpful to explore who we are as neighbors in this small planet. We need to recognize that there can be a variety of starting points, depending on people's religious traditions, that can lead us to meet, talk, listen, learn and work together.

Diana Eck provides a rich understanding of this dynamic in her definition of "pluralism." She says that "pluralism is not diversity alone, but the energetic engagement with diversity." Genuine encounter takes place, and in that encounter we don't just tolerate each other but actively seek understanding. Eck reminds us that in the world of close proximity we live in today, ignorance of one another will prove increasingly costly. Furthermore Eck holds that "pluralism is not relativism, but the encounter of commitments." We hold our religious commitments, even our deep differences, "not in isolation, but in relationship to one another." Such pluralism is based on dialogue. Eck says, "The language of pluralism is dialogue and encounter." We won't all agree, but we are committed to being together, speaking, listening and coming to an understanding of each other.

A comedy film that was produced in Egypt in 2008 provides a humorous vision for religious harmony amid a context of religious strife. Set amid the tensions of the Muslim majority and Christian minority in Egypt, the film *Hassan and Morqos* depicts two leaders, a Coptic priest and a Muslim sheikh. They are both moderates who are forced to go into hiding by extremists from their own religious communities. They end up as neighbors in the same building, become friends and form a business together. Eventually their children fall in love. With two legendary Egyptian actors playing the lead roles — Adel Imam and Omar Sharif — the film has gained high visibility and stirred controversy for honestly exposing some of the religious tensions in Egypt. In the face of the controversy, the Muslim actor Adel Imam who portrayed the Christian priest said: "I have made a work of art. That is what I can do. I have declared war using art against the extremists—against those who foment differences between us. I hope Christians and Muslims will leave the cinema and embrace and kiss one another."

Perhaps the challenge is for all of us, using whatever gifts we have, to take our stand against those who would divide us and find the way to embrace each other.

Adel Imam and Omar Sharif in Hassan and Morqos

CHAPTER 11

Sri Ramakrishna Parmahamsa
(1836-1886)

Sri Ramakrishna Parmahamsa was a Hindu sage and mystic who never wrote any articles or books. He was known for practices and experiences that many considered bizarre, but also for a "god-consciousness" that drew people to him from many religious traditions.

Raised in a poor Brahmin family (the priestly caste), the boy, known then as Gadadhar, early on evidenced a great love for nature and a passion for religious matters. He challenged customs by taking his first alms from a low-caste woman in his village rather than from another Brahmin. He followed his older brother into the Hindu priesthood, serving in a temple for the goddess Kali.

While expressing his frustration in prayer about whether Kali was a piece of stone or a living goddess, he had a life-changing religious experience he described as having waves of light coming from the deity that overwhelmed him. This experience led him to a journey of opening himself up to many expressions of divinity first within Hinduism, then extending to Islam and Christianity. He diligently practiced spiritual disciplines from these various traditions, seeking what they might teach from their faithful practice. In all these traditions he felt he could open himself up to God and have some sort of merging with the divine being.

Out of these experiences his teaching developed. He thought that revelation of God can take place at all times. "God-realization" is not monopolized by any era, country, people or religion. When religious traditions slip away from their center of passionate "god-consciousness," they become oppressive and dogmatic and lose their transformative power. All religions can be a channel for God's revelation, and therefore they are not competitive but complementary, giving visions of truth from different angles. Religions should be seen and embraced in harmony. They were not to be blended or fused into uniformity, but were diverse ways of pursing a common goal, namely communion with God. He taught, "As many faiths, so many paths." The harmony of religions was not found in uniformity but in diversity.

People of many religious traditions sought out Ramakrishna for his teaching, including Hindus, Muslims, Christians, and even atheists and humanists. His small room at the Dakshineswar temple on the edge of Calcutta became a gathering place for people of various creeds, castes, races and ages, both men and women. He didn't seek conversion but called people to deeper connection to God within the fullness of each faith.

The legacy of Ramakrishna is a mixed one. Many scholars have commented on the complex ways that his religious journey took him though forms of sexual experimentation and reflection. Some of these spiritual-sexual connections linked Ramakrishna with long-standing Hindu traditions; others led to sharp criticism from opponents and concern about his wellbeing even among his own supporters. For example, he developed an intense devotion to a female deity that, on one occasion, nearly led him to kill himself. Later, he regarded his wife as a deity. He taught about the female nature of deity in an era when this seemed shocking to some critics. On the other hand, his fearless and almost overwhelming passion for "God-consciousness" inspired great thinkers from Tolstoy to Gandhi. Ramakrishna's closest disciple was Vivekananda, who took his master's teaching to the Western world, opening up a new era of East-West religious interaction. Vivekananda participated in the Parliament of the World's Religions in 1893, introducing Ramakrishna's version of Hinduism to the larger world. Vivekananda also established a monastic order based upon the teachings of Ramakrishna.

CHAPTER 12

Hazrat Inayat Khan
(1882-1927)

Hazrat Inayat Khan grew up in a princely Muslim home that was a crossroads for many interesting people—poets, mystics, musicians and philosophers. His own family was very musical, and he developed skill in playing the Indian vina, a folk instrument. As a young person he toured the area playing folk music, especially songs with a spiritual quality. His music brought invitations to play at the courts of the Rajas, the princely rulers of Indian states under British colonial authority.

In that early cosmopolitan home Inayat also developed an appreciation for various religions and had a strong sense of the "oneness" of all faiths and creeds. In Hyderabad he met a Sufi teacher, Mohammed Abu Hasana, who helped root Inayat in the Chishti Sufi Order of Islam. Through his teacher's guidance Inayat came to a deep religious experience with God. Then when Mohammed Abu Hasana was on his death-bed he gave his disciple a charge: "Go to the Western world, my son, and unite East and West through the magic of your music." In 1910, Inayat left India for the United States.

As Inayat lectured in the U.S. and Europe he focused on the themes of divine unity, love, harmony and beauty. He was reluctant to give his teaching a name out of fear that naming it would create barriers between people who had a prejudice against Islam. For a long time, he said that great spiritual leaders never give a name to their religious views. Eventually, Inayat told people his views were part of Sufism. He emphasized the fundamental oneness of all religions. He was particularly concerned that Western religious traditions had little in the way of prayer and meditation techniques, something he called "the science of the soul." Consequently he was taught those spiritual disciplines as available to people from various traditions.

In a town near Paris Inayat developed the Universal Worship Service that is also called the "Sufi Order in the West." The worship order includes an invocation, readings from one of the holy books of the world's major religions, lighting of a candle for each tradition, including a candle for those unknown or forgotten traditions which have inspired humanity, a discourse, and a final blessing. The goal of his Universal Worship Service was to show that people from different cultures and religions share many common elements. He wanted people to be able to hear each other's scriptures and pray each other's prayers.

As Inayat taught people the "inner disciplines" of prayer and meditation to take them deeper in their religious experiences, he also taught them the importance of relating their inner spiritual journey with the larger religious community of their faith. He urged people of all faiths to engage as active members of their faith groups and their local congregations.

Growing tired from his heavy travel and lecturing schedule, Inayat was struck down by influenza in 1927. His disciples continued his practice of both being rooted in Sufi teachings and spirituality and relating in positive ways to people of other religious traditions. The incorporation of spirituality and the arts has also continued to be important for those inspired by his example and teaching.

CHAPTER 13

Juliet Garretson Hollister
(1916-2000)

Juliet Hollister was "just a nice little mother," in her words, when her life was transformed by a vision born over peanut butter sandwiches at her kitchen table. It was 1960, and the Cold War was at its height with nuclear weapons from the Soviet Union and the United States aimed threateningly at each other. "The world is in a mess," she told a friend. So she decided to do something about it. Her response to the mess she saw was to promote dialogue and understanding among the world's religions.

Hollister had earlier studied comparative religion at Columbia University and Union Theological Seminary in New York City. However, she found that the sexism in many institutions blocked her opportunities to pursue a career in theology. As she continued her studies she became convinced that all the world's major religions shared some basic humane principles, whatever their expression might be.

An opportunity to meet Eleanor Roosevelt opened the door for her dream to become a reality. She shared her vision of religious dialogue with the former First Lady, including the idea of taking a trip around the world to gain support for a "Temple of Understanding." The Temple would not be a place of religious worship, but a place of interreligious encounter and education. Mrs. Roosevelt liked the idea and described it as a "spiritual United Nations." She committed to write letters of introduction for Mrs. Hollister to use in approaching leaders such as Pope John XXIII, Albert Schweitzer, Jawaharlal Nehru of India, and UN Secretary General U Thant.

In the early 1960's, supported by Mrs. Roosevelt's letters of introduction, Mrs. Hollister and her 11-year old son began a journey around the world to promote the idea of the Temple of Understanding. The response was overwhelming. Albert Schweitzer told her, "My hopes and prayers are with you in the realization of the great Temple of Understanding, which has a profound significance… The Spirit burns in many flames." She sought not just to build an institution, but a movement of all faiths that would work for universal understanding and harmony.

The Temple of Understanding office was first opened in Washington, D.C., and Hollister began the work of organizing regional and international conferences. The first Spiritual Summit Conference was held in Calcutta, India, in 1968. Many influential religious leaders attended, including the Catholic theologian and monk Thomas Merton. A Tibetan woman also attended that conference. She invited Hollister to meet her brother in Dharamsala. Her brother was the Dalai Lama, and their friendship began a period of support and involvement of the Dalai Lama in the Temple of Understanding.

The Temple of Understanding moved to New York where it was housed at the Cathedral Church of St. John the Divine. Then in the 1990s the Temple moved into a separate office, currently located at 43rd St. in Manhattan. The Temple organized a series of summits of religious leaders to discuss problems of intolerance, injustice and religious persecution worldwide. Regional conferences were organized throughout the U.S. in conjunction with universities such as Harvard, Princeton and Cornell. The Temple of Understanding also became affiliated with the United Nations as a registered Non-Governmental Organization (NGO). In the mid-1990s the Temple secured NGO consultative status with the UN's Economic and Social Council (ECOSOC).

In the 1970s as there was an influx of religious teachers coming to the United States from Asia, the Temple of Understanding opened up many opportunities for dialogues, classes and conferences. Hollister used this historical moment to stimulate interfaith education and interaction. She kept dreaming of the Temple of Understanding as a building with wings representing the world's major religions leading to a library for learning and a pool and flame for meditation and prayer in the center. But the building kept being pushed aside in the passion for programs that brought people together.

Juliet Hollister died in 2000 at the age of 84. The Temple of Understanding has continued with the mission "to achieve peaceful coexistence among individuals, communities, and societies through interfaith education." They have especially focused on religious literacy and the most effective methods for teaching people about other religions. More recently they have been developing experiential methods of education with community visits, learning through service, and immersion experiences. Hollister's vision born over those peanut butter sandwiches has outlived her and spread around the world.

CHAPTER 14

Hans Küng
(b. 1928)

There will be no peace among the nations without peace among the religions.

There will be no peace among the religions without dialogue among the religions

Hans Küng has been a Roman Catholic theologian of astounding breadth through his prolific writing. His writings have sparked many controversies, especially when he raised theological questions about papal infallibility. That stand by Küng resulted in Pope John Paul II withdrawing Küng's official permission to teach as a theologian in Catholic universities, though he remains a priest. Coming from within the context of a church where infallible teaching is claimed in some areas, Küng has become a dramatic leading voice for ecumenical and interreligious relationship.

Küng was born in Switzerland and studied with some of the world's greatest Christian theologians in Rome and Paris. He taught theology at Tübingen University in Germany until the papal withdrawal of his official capacity to teach on behalf of the Roman Catholic Church. So he moved into an independent position with the Institute for Ecumenical Research, also at Tübingen University.

Prior to the controversy that cost him his teaching position, Küng played a major role in shaping Catholic theology. He was involved as an expert theological advisor at the groundbreaking Vatican II council in 1962-1965.

Küng became a key voice in interfaith gatherings. He held that truth is absolute, but because of the limitations of our humanity our perceptions about that truth have to be provisional. When applied in the context of interreligious relationships, he maintained his personal Christian commitment, but felt that claims of exclusivity and superiority by any religion needed to be abandoned. Religious leaders should stop competing and start cooperating. This cooperation is especially needed in the face of global issues that threaten all of humanity. For Küng ethics needs to be made a global and interreligious concern. Issues of peace, vital for the survival of humanity, necessarily entail finding the way to religious peace. Küng said, "There will be no peace among the nations without peace among the religions. There will be no peace among the religions without dialogue among the religions."

In particular there is a need for spiritual humility. Assuming that only one religion has the fullness of truth is inadequate for this time in our history according to Küng. Every religion has its problems, and every religion has something of value for the larger human community. "As a matter of fact, you have deficiencies in all religions, but you have truth in all religions. There are points where I think, for instance, Judaism or Buddhism are more constructive than the Catholic position, and vice versa."

Küng participated in the 1993 Parliament of the World's Religions. He drafted the "Declaration Toward a Global Ethic" which was adopted by the Parliament. The Declaration dealt with issues of ecology, poverty, social injustice, and aggression in the name of religion. Religious leaders must take responsibility for shaping a better global order "for the sake of human rights, freedom, justice, peace and the preservation of Earth." The Declaration included a commitment to a culture of non-violence and respect for life, to a culture of solidarity and a just economic order, to a culture of tolerance and a life of truthfulness, and to a culture of equal rights and partnership between men and women.

Küng continues to work along these lines of global interreligious cooperation in the context of the United Nations "Dialogue Among Civilizations," a project in which Küng served as one of 19 "eminent persons" pursuing the project. While some write about the "clash of civilizations," Küng has dedicated himself to finding the way for people to talk together, find common ground, and work collaboratively to solve the huge challenges that lay before the entire human community.

Chapter 15

Joseph H. Gelberman
(b. 1912)

A seminary for people of all religions? That was the idea that inspired Rabbi Joseph Gelberman after a long life of teaching within the Jewish faith. As a person who never seems to retire, he ended up establishing two such seminaries.

Gelberman was born and educated in Hungary, but later came to New York City where he graduated from the City University of New York and Yeshiva University. He worked as a therapist in mental health as well as serving as a rabbi at various synagogues in New York. He became a modern master of the Kabbalah teaching of Jewish mysticism.

In 1981 Rabbi Gelberman joined together with friends from other religions to form The New Seminary for which he became the first President. He was joined by Rev. Jon Mundy, a former Methodist minister and college professor. Father Giles Spoonhour, a Catholic priest engaging in church reformation initiatives and Swami Satchidananda, known as Sri Gurudev, a Yoga master out of the Hindu tradition also participated. The mission of the seminary was "to train interfaith ministers and spiritual counselors to serve the needs of the world community." One of the basic principles of the seminary was affirming the truth of all faiths and religious paths. The people at the seminary see interfaith interactions as a way of discovering the work of God's Spirit in the world and participating in the divine healing of the world through spiritual awakening. The grand vision had small beginnings as they first held classes in the basement of a building in Greenwich Village. Since the founding of the seminary 2,000 "interfaith ministers" have graduated, trained to perform interfaith religious services: designing rituals and worship services, teaching and counseling.

In 1998 Rabbi Gelberman stepped down as President of the New Seminary, but he was still eager to continue his teaching. So he took the vision of The New Seminary and internationalized it. He established the All-Faiths Seminary International, based in New York with branches in Canada, Japan, China and Europe. These schools have helped create a new type of religious leader able to work in different religious contexts as well as outside specific houses of worship.

❓ Discussion Questions
Chapters 10-15

When you think of religious harmony, do you think of all religions being different roads to one Truth or to one God? Or do you think there are significant differences at the basic level of religions and that harmony must be established at the level of personal respect and humility? How would you go about building a foundation for communication and relationship with someone who has a different view about the basis for religious harmony?

Diana Eck says that "pluralism is not diversity alone, but the energetic engagement with diversity." She says "pluralism is not relativism, but the encounter of commitments." She also says "The language of pluralism is dialogue and encounter." In Eck's view of interfaith pluralism we won't all agree, but we are committed to being together, speaking, listening and coming to understanding of each other. What do you think of this understanding of pluralism? Is it helpful? If so, in what way? Are there any problems or limitations you see?

Hazrat Inayat Khan developed a Universal Worship Service, and the seminaries established by Joseph Gelberman prepare students to be leaders for interreligious worship experiences. What do you think about people of different religions actually sharing in a worship experience together? Is genuine shared worship possible for people from different faiths? Does multi-religious worship diminish or negate the importance of worship in one's own faith tradition? Does shared worship move to an insipid blandness of "the lowest common denominator"? What might be the most helpful way you can envision for people of different religions to share a worship experience together?

Hans Küng said, "As a matter of fact, you have deficiencies in all religions, but you have truth in all religions." What do you think are some of the strengths in your religion, the dimensions of truth that are especially well stated or lived out in the practices of your religious community? What do you think are some of the deficiencies or blind spots common in both the articulation and the practices of your faith? What have you noticed as strengths in other religions that challenge you at the point of a deficiency in your own faith?

Hans Küng also said, "There will be no peace among the nations without peace among the religions." Should there be peace among the religions? What would peace among the religions look like? What local steps could you as an individual take for peace among the religions? What local steps could your congregation take?

CHAPTER 16

Learning From Other Religions
Maybe We Don't Have All the Answers

There is a story in Christian tradition, attributed to John of Damascus, about St. Josaphat, the son of an Indian king who persecuted Christians. A holy man made a prophecy that one day Josaphat himself would become a Christian. To keep his son from this fate the king locked up Josaphat. But, eventually a monk from Mt. Sinai was traveling through the region as a merchant offering "a pearl of great price." This monk, by the name of Barlaam, drew out the young man and converted him to Christianity. After being baptized, Josaphat renounced all his possessions including his throne. He went to the desert with Barlaam and sought the spiritual life of a monk.

It's an interesting story, but it also is a fascinating example of interfaith dialogue and learning. Stories from one tradition speak to another and are then reformulated within the context of the other religion. The story of Josaphat and Barlaam was a very inspirational and influential one during the Middle Ages in both the Eastern and Western Churches. Historical research has traced it to a Georgian Orthodox monk living on Mount Athos in Greece in the 11th Century. From him the story was circulated in both Greek and Latin, then made its way into many vernacular translations. But this Georgian monk wasn't the originator of the tale.

There is a Muslim story that is almost identical, which in turn appears to have been an adaptation from a Manichean story found in Western Asia. That story goes back to the story of Siddhartha Gautama, the Hindu prince who renounced his royal family, wealth and power to follow the path of spiritual enlightenment. When he sat under the Bodhi tree and received enlightenment, he was called a *Bodhisattva*. As the story migrated across languages and cultures *Bodhisattva* became *Bodisaf* in Manichee, then *Yudasaf* in Arabic, *Lodasaph* in Georgia, *Ioasaph* in Greek and finally *Josaphat* in Latin. So a story that was foundational to Buddhism inspired people from other religions who made it their own, in Manicheanism, Islam, Orthodox Christianity and Catholic Christianity. Learning from people of other religions is neither new nor unusual.

The story of Barlaam and Josaphat has continued in modern times. The Russian Christian Leo Tolstoy wrote about this story in his *Confessions*. The radical commitment of Josaphat inspired Tolstoy's own conversion to following Christ. When the Hindu lawyer Mohandas Gandhi discovered the writings of Tolstoy, he was inspired by the message of nonviolence in Jesus as related by Tolstoy. That Christian message then helped Gandhi to access more deeply some of the traditions in his own faith for the practice of nonviolence. Then the African-American Baptist Christian, Martin Luther King, Jr., found in the writings of the Hindu Gandhi the method for practicing the teachings of Jesus from the Sermon on the Mount in the context of the systemic oppression of black people in the American South. This migration of ideas and inspiration across religious identities continued. Robert Ellsberg in his book *All Saints* relates the story of Josaphat and Barlaam and its travels through religions, cultures and time. Rather than reject the characters in this story as mere legend, Ellsberg suggests that we celebrate them as patron saints for interreligious dialogue.

Many people have gained important new insights from faiths beyond their own — without ever giving up their original faith. Some have taken on the task of teaching about different religions, not to encourage conversions but to bring deeper understanding and appreciation of those who think, feel and live within differing religious paradigms. The entire academic discipline called Comparative Religion has developed to support broader religious understanding. In various ways, interfaith heroes challenge us to learn from others, perhaps even surprisingly enriching our own faith in the process.

Chapter 17

Zheng He
(1371-1433)

Six hundred years ago, one of the greatest human explorers sailed the seas. He was the Chinese Admiral Zheng He who sailed with a massive fleet on seven trading voyages from 1405 to 1433. These voyages were unprecedented in size, organization, navigational technology and financial cost. One fleet was estimated to include some 300 ships to carry his army and goods for trade. The fleets of Zheng He traveled throughout South East Asia, through what is now Indonesia, around India, to the Arabian Peninsula, the Persian Gulf, the Red Sea and down the East Coast of Africa. Just a few years before Henry the Navigator was beginning the European explorations along the coast of Africa starting from the west, Zheng He was exploring Africa from the east. The Chinese admiral visited regions that now encompass over thirty Asian and African nations.

Growing up in the central Asian province of Yunnan, Zheng He was swept up into the internal dynastic conflicts and political intrigues of China. He was captured by Ming Dynasty forces as they overthrew the Yuan Dynasty. He was taken from Yunnan to Nanjing, castrated, and eventually entered into the imperial service as a body guard. His leadership skills became apparent to Prince Zhu Di in the struggle for power, and Zheng He quickly rose in the ranks. When Zhu Di became the

Yongle Emperor, he raised Zheng He to the position of Grand Eunuch as one of his most trusted advisors. When the Emperor wanted to launch exploration of the seas, Zheng He was the obvious choice to lead the envisioned voyages.

Zheng He was born into the Muslim faith, the predominant religion in Yunnan. From childhood he studied Islam. His father and grandfather made the *hajj* pilgrimage to Mecca, igniting the curiosity in Zheng He for distant lands. Over the years, Zheng augmented his military and navigational studies by studying other religions, particularly Confucianism and Buddhism, which were major shapers of the Chinese culture. He developed an approach to religious tolerance, based on his education, and put this method into practice as he encountered people of different faiths in his travels. Some might call his approach syncretistic today, though he used his understanding to develop empathetic connections between himself and those he met. In Sri Lanka, also known as Ceylon, he made offerings at a Buddhist mountain temple. In honor of the meeting of the people of differing faiths, Zheng He and local residents set up a monument honoring Buddha, Allah and Vishnu. In China's Jujian province, Zheng He set up a pillar to the Taoist goddess Tian Fei as a way to offer prayers for the safety of his sailors, who were drawn from many faiths. Despite his openness to learn about and interact collegially with other religions, Zheng He and many of his Chinese Muslim sailors aided the spread of Islam in South East Asia. They frequented mosques, propagated their faith, and sometimes left communities of Chinese Muslims in Java, the Malay Peninsula and the Philippines.

Zheng He died during his last voyage and probably was buried at sea as was traditional for Chinese admirals. There is a huge tomb in China built in Islamic style to honor him, but it stands empty. After his death the Chinese government decided the naval expeditions were not cost effective, and in a few years the major economic focus for China was shifted to building the Great Wall.

Zheng He's legacy has been a matter of controversy in Asia. China celebrates his travels and presents him as a peaceful diplomat in contrast with the rapaciousness of the colonial powers. The Chinese government has minimized Zheng He's Muslim faith, while ethnic Chinese living in Indonesia celebrate Zheng He as a hero bridging the lands and cultures of the two countries. Indonesian Muslims, however, have been suspicious of the Chinese muting of the Admiral's religion, fearing an anti-Islamic sentiment from China. In an era when the lines of definition and division between religions have been a source of conflict, the interpretation of Zheng's legacy and identity is a contrast to the more relaxed and syncretistic spirit of the Admiral's era. Perhaps something in his legacy could help lead the way to reconciliation along the ethnic and religious rifts in places like Indonesia and China.

Chapter 18

Kabir
(1398-1448)

O servant, where dost thou seek Me?
O servant, where dost thou seek Me?
Lo ! I am beside thee.
I am neither in temple nor in mosque:
I am neither in Kaaba nor in Kailash:
Neither am I in rites and ceremonies,
nor in Yoga and renunciation.
If thou art a true seeker, thou shalt at once see Me:
thou shalt meet Me in a moment of time.
Kabir says, ' O Sadhu ! God is the breath of all breath.'

Kabir's life is shrouded in legend and conflicting stories, so any attempt to construct a coherent account is a bold and presumptuous exercise. Because Kabir has so many fascinating interreligious dimensions to his life and work, however, the effort must be made.

He was born in 1398 or 1440, and died in 1448 or 1518. He lived for more than 50 years or more than 100 years, so the basic facts are confusing to say the least. Whatever the case, we have his poetry — poetry that has spoken powerfully to the hearts of people in a variety of cultures and religious traditions from Hinduism and Islam to Christianity and Buddhism. The Sikhs have incorporated some of his poetry into their Scriptures and revere him as they do their ten Gurus.

According to most accounts Kabir, whose name has Muslim roots, was an orphan adopted by a childless Muslim couple who were weavers. Kabir worked as a weaver all his life, anchoring his mystical life in the realities of a tradesman. He believed that one must lead a balanced life including work and contemplation, so he lived simply and spent much of his life in the ordinary experience of raising a family.

Kabir's first interfaith action was to become a disciple of a Hindu mystic by the name of Ramananda. Ramananda accepted students of all castes, unusual in his day, and challenged them to devotion to Vishnu as the personal aspect of the Divine. Kabir as a child hid near the river Ganges to catch the Master during his early morning walk. According to tradition, one became a disciple by having a Guru say the name of God over the would-be disciple, so Kabir grabbed Ramananda's big toe, and the Guru called out the name of God in surprise. When Ramananda saw Kabir's name written on his hand in Arabic, he knew the child was a Muslim. Yet Ramananda still took him on as a student, provoking some of his Hindu students to leave in protest.

Kabir became associated with a loose group of teachers called the *Sant Mat*. The *Sant Mat* lived in north India and taught a form of egalitarianism that in a wide variety of ways challenged the caste system in Hinduism. They sought to transcend the religious differences between Hinduism and Islam. Kabir also was influenced by the teachings of Buddhist Tantrism. Salvation for him involved a process of bringing into union the personal soul with God, and in that quest he utilized many of the Sufi mystical practices. He also embraced the teachings of reincarnation and karma from Hinduism. He saw no separation between the natural and supernatural worlds, rather everything was part of the creative "Play of the Eternal Lover." Though influenced by so many traditions, he refused to align himself with any one faith. He said he was "at once the child of Allah and of Ram." He would question and challenge any religious teaching until he could validate it through his own experience.

Officials from all the religions in India criticized Kabir, and one king banished him from his region. At the same time orthodox writers in each of those religious traditions respected Kabir and recited his poetry. He had no patience with hypocrisy in any religion, and could be very critical. He challenged people to develop an internal devotion to God and to spiritual honesty, rather than what he saw as stale rituals and traditions. He called for an inner reformation of all religion. Because the inner relationship with God was accessible to all, God was more accessible to the "washerwoman and carpenter" than to the self-righteous holy man. Such teaching had him branded as a heretic by the orthodox traditions.

Kabir's poetry was exuberant, spontaneous love poetry toward God. He chose to make his poetry accessible to ordinary people, composing in Hindi, the language of the masses, rather than Sanskrit. He was illiterate, so his poems were composed and handed down orally. Kabir drew extensively from religious images in both Islam and Hinduism in his writings. Many times he put his poems to music, for he was also skilled as a musician.

Even the legend of his death speaks of interreligious reconciliation. The story goes that his Muslim and Hindu followers fought over his body and the burial rights. Muslims bury their dead, while Hindus cremate theirs. When the fighting factions opened the coffin, they found no body. Instead there was a small blank book in which all the Hindus and Muslims together wrote down as many of the sayings of Kabir as they could remember. Another version of the legend says they found flowers inside the coffin. The Muslims buried half the flowers while the Hindus burned the other half. Whatever the version, both sides viewed what happened as a miracle of divine intervention for religious reconciliation.

Chapter 19

Evelyn Underhill
(1875-1941)

You don't have to be peculiar to find God.

The writings of Evelyn Underhill dominated discussions about the spiritual life in the first half of the 20th Century. Her book *Mysticism*, published in 1911, was unmatched in publishing success for over forty years. Born in England in 1875, she had mystical experiences in her childhood. These experiences prompted a life-long journey of spiritual exploration, research, writing and discovery. She was an agnostic early on, raised in a non-religious family. Eventually her spiritual quest drew her to the Anglican Church, particularly the Anglo-Catholic wing of the Church.

Though she never earned a doctoral degree herself, she became the first woman to lecture clergy in the Church of England and then received an honorary Doctorate of Divinity from Aberdeen University. She was a frequent lecturer at English colleges and universities, often the first woman to do so in some settings. Besides her scholarly work on mysticism and her writings about spirituality, she was a novelist and a poet. In her novels she explored the connections between the world of the spirit and our ordinary experiences, seeing their inseparability and the way divine radiance can bathe our reality. She especially taught that ordinary people could open themselves up to the divine, something that drew so many of those ordinary people to her writings. She wrote, "You don't have to be peculiar to find God."

As she studied mysticism Underhill entered into a special collaboration with the Indian Hindu mystic Rabindranath Tagore (featured in *Interfaith Heroes*). They not only worked together as scholars, but Underhill opened herself to learn from the mystical traditions and practices of a teacher from another religion, while maintaining strongly her own Christian spirituality. Together Underhill and Tagore studied the Muslim mystical poet Kabir. Tagore translated *100 Poems of Kabir* into English while Underhill wrote an extensive introduction. Underhill wrote to Tagore afterward, "This is the first time I have had the privilege of being with one who is a Master in the things I care so much about but know so little of as yet; and I understand now something of what your writers mean when they insist on the necessity and value of the personal teacher and the fact that he gives something which the learner cannot get in any other way. It has been like hearing the language of which I barely know the alphabet, spoken perfectly."

In her last major work Underhill turned for mysticism to the experience of corporate worship. Her book *Worship* described, analyzed and explored the basic characteristics of worship such as ritual, symbol, sacrifice and sacrament. As with mysticism, she remained rooted in her Christian faith, but she was able to explore worship within the various traditions of Christianity such as Orthodoxy, Anglicanism, Catholicism and Reformed Protestantism. She also studied worship within Judaism, learning from another tradition to shed light on her own.

For Underhill spiritual life begins with the love of God. Everything follows from that, including how we relate to others. For her the love of neighbor is a corollary of the love of God, not its equivalent. So out of her deep mystical relationship with God, she engaged the world in love, including people of other faiths who had things to teach her.

Chapter 20

Simone Weil

(1909-1943)

Simone Weil was born in Paris to wealthy agnostic parents of Jewish ancestry. From childhood she suffered from poor health, eventually succumbing to tuberculosis at the age of 34, in part because she refused to eat more than the official French war ration when she was ill. But in her brief life she became a bright light for spirituality and social activism.

Weil was a brilliant student, but she was even more impassioned about issues of social injustice. At the age of 6 she refused to eat sugar in solidarity with suffering troops in World War I. Then at 10 she said she was a Bolshevik and as a teenager was active in workers demonstrations for trade unions, earning the nickname "The Red Virgin." After Weil became a teacher, she continued her activism both in writing and in the streets. At one point she took a year off from teaching to work in factories incognito to help understand the experiences of the working class. Her poor health quickly put an end to this experiment.

Though a pacifist and an anarchist in conviction she fought in the Spanish Civil War on the Republican side. She was known for her clumsiness and was seriously burned in a cooking accident. Weil went to Assisi to recover, and there in 1937 she experienced a religious conversion. She prayed for the first time in her life amid an ecstatic experience in the same church where Saint Francis had prayed. She embraced Roman Catholicism, but stopped short of baptism, for she felt the Catholic Church was in too much need of reformation. Finding God's will for her life became her new passion, not replacing her earlier social passions, but becoming the larger context for them.

Weil received spiritual direction from a Dominican friar and learned much from the Catholic author Gustave Thibon. She was especially rooted in neo-Platonic thinking in her spiritual writings. Yet her spiritual curiosity took her far. She learned Sanskrit to read the Bhagavad Gita. She studied Mahayana Buddhism and the ancient Greek and Egyptian mystery religions. She believed that each religion, when we are within it, is true. But she was opposed to religious syncretism. She saw a blending of religions as diminishing the particularity of each tradition and the truth of that path to God. Though she learned from other faiths, she plunged deeper into her own Catholicism. For Weil truth was deeply personal and could only be approached through deep introspection. She wrote intensely about spirituality, mysticism, beauty and social struggle. Her writings sought to develop the intellectual consequences of the religious experiences she was having.

When the Nazis occupied France, Simone Weil joined the French Resistance working in England. The toll of the work was more than her frail condition could handle, and she contracted tuberculosis that led to her death in a sanatorium.

Chapter 21

Mohandas Gandhi, Martin Luther King, Jr. and Aung San Suu Kyi
(1869-1948)   (1929-1968)   (b. 1945)

The way of nonviolence leads to redemption and the creation of the beloved community.
   —Martin Luther King, Jr.

Throughout the 20th Century and into the 21st Century a movement developed that has changed the political maps of the world. It is a movement that has touched every continent. The movement is focused around the principles of nonviolent struggle to bring justice and freedom to people who have been experiencing oppression. The thread weaving together the center of this movement is people acting passionately and explicitly out of their religious beliefs, yet at the same time learning at their very core from people of other faiths.

The three people who most clearly embody this tradition through history are Mohandas Gandhi, Martin Luther King, Jr. and Aung San Suu Kyi, a Hindu, a Christian and a Buddhist. This trio of heroes are known for their dramatic actions and leadership in situations of great oppression (see *Interfaith Heroes* chapters 12 and 21 for more about Gandhi and King), but here we will look deeper at how they learned from believers and practitioners of other religions in the shaping of their own beliefs and actions.

Mohandas Gandhi, also known by his honorific title Mahatma, was a Hindu Indian. Gandhi's ideas were initially shaped while he was a law student in London. He came across Leo Tolstoy's *The Kingdom of God is Within You*, which Gandhi said, "overwhelmed me." This book came out of Tolstoy's own spiritual revolution in his 50s when the Christian writer looked to the transformation of all of society through the inner moral revolution that came from following the teachings of Jesus. Confronting the failure of Christians to acknowledge "the law of non-resistance to evil by violence" was at the center of Tolstoy's work. Tolstoy believed the Church had perverted the teachings of Jesus. Instead, Christians should follow the law of love and reject violence. *The Kingdom of God is Within You* was banned by the Russian censors, but it was published in other countries in Europe. As Gandhi read it, he said, "Before the independent thinking, profound morality, and the truthfulness of this book, all the books given me … paled into insignificance."

Tolstoy's writing helped Gandhi crystallize his own thinking. He wrote about Tolstoy's book, "It's reading cured me of my skepticism and made me a firm believer in *ahimsa* (nonviolence)." Furthermore, while reading this Christian's treatment of nonviolence Gandhi was liberated from a narrow orthodoxy in Hinduism, including the injustices of untouchability, even as Tolstoy had been from narrow views of Christianity. Tolstoy rooted his nonviolence in the law of love, which Gandhi recognized in every religion, including his own Hindu faith. Gandhi initiated a correspondence with Tolstoy which continued until the latter's death in 1910. In his last letter to Gandhi, Tolstoy wrote, "Your activity is the most essential work, the most important of all the work now being done in the world."

While influenced and inspired by Tolstoy's Christian nonresistance, Gandhi took the teachings further in both theory and practice. Gandhi did not teach *nonresistance* to evil but rather *nonviolent resistance*. He also thought more positively about the state than Tolstoy did. Gandhi engaged in political struggle that brought about political change and social reformation, whereas Tolstoy had withdrawn to his farm and the private practice of his morality.

After Gandhi's nonviolent campaigns with the Indians in South Africa and against the British Empire in his native India, independence was finally achieved for India in 1947. Meanwhile, African-Americans in the United States were seeking ways to resist the oppressions of racial segregation in the American South. A young seminary student named Martin Luther King, Jr. almost despaired that the power of love could deal with the vast social problems on his heart, including the oppression of black people in racist America. Then he found works on the life and teachings of Gandhi, especially the biography written by E. Stanley Jones. "As I delved deeper into the philosophy of Gandhi," King wrote, "my skepticism concerning the power of love gradually diminished, and I came to see for the first time that the Christian doctrine of love operating through the Gandhian method of nonviolence was one of the most potent weapons available to oppressed people in their struggle for freedom." King was ready to move from despair into liberating action.

During the Montgomery bus boycott of 1954, King said, "Christ furnished the spirit and motivation, while Gandhi furnished the method." King frequently referred to Gandhi's philosophy and example as he trained the activists in Montgomery and preached from his pulpit every Sunday. Some of the key points King gathered from Gandhi in his practice of nonviolence included that the method was not for cowards in that it called for resistance. Suffering that was willingly embraced could be redemptive, the secret power within nonviolence. Furthermore, nonviolence did not seek to defeat or humiliate the opponent but rather to understand and even win the opponent's friendship. Gandhi also taught King not to personalize the attacks against evil, to focus on the forces of injustice, not the people acting out through those forces. A key part of religious nonviolence for both Gandhi and King, which is not accepted by all practitioners of nonviolent struggle, was that nonviolent resistance rejects the internal violence of the spirit as well as external physical violence.

In 1959 Dr. King traveled to India. He met with the followers of Gandhi in their continuing struggles for justice and shaping the government of India. He was particularly moved by the lack of rancor after the independence struggle. Violent revolutions leave an aftermath of bitterness and hatred, but King saw that "the way of nonviolence leads to redemption and the creation of the beloved community." King continued to see with eyes of both the learner and the prophet. He was moved by the desperate poverty he saw and affirmed the global connection of all people in the struggle for justice. He also noted how the Indian government, growing out of the history of Gandhi's advocacy for justice for the untouchables, had developed programs for special treatment to help these victims of centuries of discrimination leap forward politically and socially. He saw this as a moral responsibility for governments to seize an opportunity to profoundly address the damages of discrimination. Perhaps this insight was the birth of efforts at affirmative action in the U.S.

Aung San Suu Kyi rose to prominence during the brief democracy uprising in Burma in 1988. (Burma's name was changed formally by the military dictatorship to Myanmar, but many democracy advocates, ethnic minorities and the U.S. government still refer to the country as Burma.) During the month of demonstrations before the massive military crackdown that re-imposed military dominance Suu Kyi (pronounced *sue she*) was the main speaker, galvanizing the crowds with her speeches and her presence.

Aung San Suu Kyi bears the name of her father, Aung San, the general who led the independence struggle in Burma against the British. On the verge of independence Aung San was assassinated when his daughter was 2 years old, but he remains to this day a hero in the hearts of most Burmese. Until 1988 Suu Kyi had a relatively quiet life, growing up in a well-to-do family that lived in India and England. She studied at Oxford, married a British scholar and became a scholar herself while raising a family.

Her widowed mother served as Burma's ambassador to India during Suu Kyi's high school and early college years. There she was exposed to the life and philosophy of Mahatma Gandhi. She explored his work related to the anti-colonial struggle, comparing Gandhi to her honored father. In her studies she noted especially how remaining in his Hindu tradition nevertheless allowed Gandhi the intellectual flexibility to learn from and accept elements of other traditions that could fit into his ethical understanding and strengthen his work. As a scholar, then as a democracy activist, Suu Kyi took the teachings of nonviolent resistance in Gandhi and King and welded them into the non-elitist philosophy of Buddhism to build a broad-based movement for freedom. She also connected to Buddhist teachings about education, often focused in the monastery, as the way to come to enlightenment.

A central lesson Suu Kyi learned from Gandhi was how to deal with fear. In facing the overwhelming might and brutality of the Burmese military, dealing with fear would be a critical challenge, a challenge picked up in the title of her book *Freedom from Fear*. Jawaharlal Nehru's description of Gandhi was especially meaningful to her: "The essence of his teaching was fearlessness and truth, and action allied to these, always keeping the welfare of the masses in view." Looking at the struggles of her own people she wrote, "A people who would build a nation in which strong, democratic institutions are firmly established as a guarantee against state-induced power must first learn to liberate their own minds from apathy and fear." Another Hindu, Tagore (featured in *Interfaith Heroes*) gave her a special image in his poem *Gitanjali* in which he spoke of a state, "….where the mind is without fear and the head is held high."

In an action that has become legendary for the people of Burma and other nonviolent activists around the world Suu Kyi directly confronted the Burmese Army. Defying a military ban on her political activity, she was on a campaign tour for the parliamentary election called by the military, running as a candidate with her National League for Democracy. Soldiers under the command of a captain knelt down to take aim at her. Suu Kyi motioned her followers to get off to the side of the road while she continued walking straight toward the guns aimed at her. "It seemed so much simpler to provide them with a single target than to bring everyone else in," she explained. The order to fire was halted, and she walked through the line of soldiers. In July, 1989 Suu Kyi was arrested. Despite having their leader under detention for months, the NLD overwhelmingly won the election in May 1990, but the military refused to let the elected parliamentarians be seated. Hundreds of NLD members were arrested and others fled into exile.

Under house arrest since 1989 with periodic short releases, Aung San Suu Kyi has remained steadfast and fearless in her nonviolent discipline and call for a democratic government in Burma. She has repeatedly cited the works and examples of Mahatma Gandhi and Martin Luther King, Jr. in her speeches and writings. Drawing upon the teachings of this Hindu and this Christian, she developed her own version of nonviolent action compatible with Buddhist spirituality.

CHAPTER 22

E. Stanley Jones
(1884-1973)

Peace is a by-product of conditions out of which peace naturally comes.

A Christian missionary evangelist as an interfaith hero? A man who held open-air evangelistic meetings with thousands of people in a predominantly non-Christian country, called the "Billy Graham of India," as a role model in learning from other faiths?

Yes, E. Stanley Jones is such a paradoxical hero and role model.

Eli Stanley Jones was born in Baltimore, Maryland. After finishing his college education he went to India as a missionary with the Methodist Episcopal Church. He began working among the very low castes, including those now called the Dalits. In time he drew the attention of the intelligentsia and was invited to speak to students at universities across India. He was very popular as a speaker, for he did not attack Hinduism, Buddhism, Islam, or any other religion in India.

Instead he sought to separate the Jesus of the gospels from enculturation in forms of Western civilization. He said, "The way of Jesus should be—but often isn't—the way of Christianity. Western civilization is only partly Christianized."

The meeting between Jones and Gandhi had a profound impact on the Christian missionary. They became close friends, and Jones became close to the Nehru family and others in the movement for Indian independence. Jones eventually wrote a biography of the Hindu Indian activist. Jones' biography of Gandhi was the initial link between Gandhi and Martin Luther King, Jr. King said that it was while reading Jones' biography that he became convinced to adopt a strict non-violent method in the struggle for civil rights.

Gandhi also challenged Jones about the Western forms of Christianity and the need for greater respect of the strengths of Indian culture and character. As Jones wrestled with Gandhi's challenge, his own missionary understanding and practice was refined. He wrote *The Christ of the Indian Road*, which sold over a million copies. He then founded the first Christian Ashram, seeking to express the Christian faith through Indian cultural forms while maintaining a passionate and articulate orthodox Christian message, a process he called "indigenization."

Jones initiated round-table conferences that brought Christians and and non-Christians together to discuss how religion can improve life. He envisioned a broader gathering, a Round-Table of nations, speaking about this dream 30 years before the founding of the United Nations. Through his interreligious dialogue and connection with leaders in the Indian independence movement, Jones helped influence the shapers of the new constitution of India to include religious freedom as a fundamental component of the nation.

Later in his ministry he traveled around the world speaking about peace and international understanding. He said, "Peace is a by-product of conditions out of which peace naturally comes. If reconciliation is God's chief business, it is ours—between man and God, between man and himself, and between man and man." His efforts of reconciliation in Africa, Asia and between Japan and the United States earned him a nomination for the Nobel Peace Price. In Japan he was hailed as "The Apostle of Peace."

E. Stanley Jones was extremely vigorous physically. He kept a heavy travel and speaking schedule and also wrote 26 books. He died at the age of 88 shortly after giving another speech, this time from a wheel chair following a stroke. As a Methodist publication put it, he was a "missionary extraordinary," but he also was willing to be challenged by those of other faiths, learn from them, and be shaped by the dialog with those who believed differently.

Chapter 23

Thomas Merton
(1915-1968)

All that is true, by whomever it is said, is from the Holy Spirit.

Paradox is at the heart of Zen Buddhism, which was part of what drew the Christian monk Thomas Merton deep into the study of Buddhism and other religions of Asia. The paradox was there at the beginning of his journey, even before Merton became a Christian. Born in France to an international family, Merton moved to the U.S. as a child. He was educated in France, England and the United States. It was at Columbia University that he marked three milestones: He participated in his first peace actions, demonstrating against the Italian invasion of Ethiopia. He plunged into a spiritual search that led to his conversion to Catholicism. And paradoxically, before he became a Christian, he met a Hindu mystic, Bramachari, who advised Merton not to read Hindu scriptures in his spiritual journey but to explore his own

Christian tradition of mysticism beginning with Augustine and Thomas á Kempis.

After his conversion Merton initially had little concern for other forms of Christianity, and certainly none for other religions. Following a stumbling search for his vocation within the church, Merton joined the Abbey of Our Lady of Gethsemani in Kentucky and became a part of the strict Trappist order of monks. He wrote prolifically after the surprising success of his early autobiography, *Seven Storey Mountain*, in 1948. Merton was later embarrassed by the religious exclusivism in his early works and apologized for the lack of "ecumenical spirit." As he matured, Merton taught young monks about contemplation, struggling through his own tendencies to intellectualize as he sought to enter into the contemplative practice and spirit.

In the 1950s Merton began a long-term study of other religions: Hinduism, Taoism, Confucianism, Islam and especially Zen Buddhism. He was inspired by the challenge of Gandhi that one can find the deeper roots of one's own religious tradition by becoming immersed in other religions and then returning "home" to see one's own tradition with a transformed consciousness and awareness. Merton contacted the Japanese Zen scholar D.T. Suzuki who was popularizing Zen in the West, and they began a long discussion on the similarities and differences between Zen Buddhism and Christianity. Merton launched his interfaith encounters with humility, expressing his approach to Suzuki: "I will not be so foolish as to pretend to you that I understand Zen. To be frank, I hardly understand Christianity." Yet Suzuki was impressed by Merton's profound grasp of both Zen and Christianity. Eventually Merton began to frame his quest as wanting "to become as good a Buddhist as I can" because only with immersion inside the perspective and experience of another faith could he learn in depth that which would drive him deeper into his own Christianity. He found the 4th Century Christian writer Ambrose affirming this perspective saying, "All that is true, by whomever it is said, is from the Holy

Spirit." Ambrose echoed the Buddhist teacher Bankei who said, "The further one enters into truth, the deeper it is."

Merton held fast to his Christian beliefs, but felt the contemporary Church had to take seriously the reality of the diverse religions in the world. In fact, for him religious dialogue was a spiritual necessity in the nuclear age because the West needed "the spiritual heritage of the East" or else the West would "hasten the tragedy that threatens man and his civilizations." The opening of the Catholic Church to dialogue and collaboration with other religions through the Second Vatican Council gave formal approval for what Merton was already doing. Merton found the connection point between Christianity and Buddhism not in doctrines and intellectual formulas but in the rejection of the false self and direct experience through contemplation of where God is in emptiness and compassion.

In the last decade of his life Merton engaged in extensive written correspondence with interfaith friends around the world including Abdul Aziz, John Wu, Amiya Chakravarty, Abraham Heschel, D.T. Suzuki, Thich Nhat Hanh and Dona Luisa Coomaraswamy. In these letters he showed a desire to learn from others, not so much in matters of doctrines in which the difference of religion were apparent, but in religious practice and religious experience. He found common ground and in some cases common language that could bind him with his friends of other faiths through their shared experiences of the "God behind God" encountered in the silence of meditation and mystical experience. He also found commonality in the motivation from these spiritual experiencing driving one toward the world in compassionate action. Seeing the inner-workings of spiritual practice and compassionate action in Taoism, Islamic Sufism, Buddhism and Hinduism helped him understand and refine his own Catholic spirituality and action in the world.

Another paradox that Merton uncovered was that his withdrawal from the world, even living as a hermit on the grounds of Gethsemani for years, drove him toward the world. He found the compassion of God in contemplation that empowered his insights to speak to the sufferings of the world, particularly poverty, racism and war. Though many social and peace activists urged him to leave the monastery, he knew that the power of his writings was fueled by the disciplines of contemplation.

The culmination of Thomas Merton's interreligious journey was a trip to Asia in 1968. He met the Dalai Lama, and they quickly developed a deep friendship. The Dalai Lama said of Merton, "I could see that he was a truly humble and deeply spiritual man. This was the first time I had been struck by such a feeling of spirituality by anyone who professed Christianity." The Buddhist leader said Merton opened his eyes to the truth that Tibetan Buddhism does not hold the world's only truth. The spiritual discovery was going both ways. Later in a Buddhist temple in Ceylon (now Sri Lanka) Merton had his last mystical experience of which he said, "I have now seen and have pierced through the surface and have got beyond the shadow and the disguise." For Merton religious dialogue took place primarily at the experiential and mystical level and only secondarily at the intellectual and academic.

Paradox marked Merton's death. He died by accidental electrocution while taking a brief break from a conference on Buddhism in Thailand. He had stepped out of the bath, evidently stumbled and grabbed a fan with a faulty electrical cord. His body was flown back to the U.S. in a B-52 bomber carrying remains of American soldiers killed in Vietnam, a war he had strongly opposed. Though his life was cut short, the challenge of Merton's spiritual journey remains.

Chapter 24

Karen Armstrong and Bruce Feiler
(b. 1944)   (b.1964)

So the question is not whether God can bring peace into the world.
The question is: Can we?

Two authors have been especially noteworthy in recent years for advancing the cause of interfaith understanding through their writings. Karen Armstrong has written scholarly books in such a readable way that a broader public can access them. Bruce Feiler has written spiritual travelogues that invite the reader into his own journey of both geography and soul.

Armstrong's journey took her from the convent to the university to global media, and from faith to unbelief to a renewed faith that she calls "freelance monotheism." Born in Britain, Armstrong joined the Society of the Holy Child Jesus as a teenager, eventually becoming a nun. She entered into academic circles both as a student and teacher in English, but severe health problems made that course difficult for her. Her faith had eroded to the point she actually became hostile to religion. Then in 1984 she was sent to Jerusalem to do a religious documentary on St. Paul, partly to debunk religion, but being in Jerusalem transformed her attitude. Her yearning for the transcendent was reawakened in this city holy to the three Abrahamic faiths.

As Armstrong explored Judaism, Christianity and Islam she began to focus on what unites the faiths. She started to write books on comparative religion, including her highly successful *A History of God*. She saw the key to religion not in belief but in behavior. She writes, "The one and only test of a valid religious idea ... was that it must lead directly to practical compassion." For her the Golden Rule as expressed in the various faiths is a common thread that can direct all people.

The challenge of how to live in a constructive relationship with other faiths has been with human societies throughout history. Armstrong analyzes the dynamics of religious fundamentalism in different religions, but calls for something deeper from within each of them. "We need to create a new narrative, get out of the rat-run of hatred, chauvinism and defensiveness; and make the authentic voice of religion a power in the world that is conducive to peace."

Armstrong has taught at a rabbinical school, addressed Islamic conferences because of her perceived "more objective" view of Islam as a Westerner, and appeared frequently in documentaries about religion on television. Though some critics charge her with using different standards to evaluate Judaism and Christianity on the one hand than she does with Islam on the other, her work has made many world religions accessible to readers struggling to understand people whose beliefs are different from their own. Her recent works on the Buddha have taken her beyond the Abrahamic faiths, but still she is exploring how to bring compassionate action out of the heart of religion. As the Roosevelt Institute put it when awarding her the Freedom of Worship Award in 2008, Armstrong has become "a significant voice, seeking mutual understanding in times of turbulence, confrontation and violence among religious groups." The Institute praised her for "her personal dedication to the ideal that peace can be found in religious understanding, for her teachings on compassion, and her appreciation for the positive sources of spirituality."

Bruce Feiler has been more of a free-lance journalist and writer. His books *Walking the Bible* and *Abraham: A Journey to the Heart of Three Faiths* are travelogues that weave together the ancient and contemporary stories with his own personal journey toward understanding and faith. Feiler was born to a Jewish family in the American South, but as the reader follows Feiler's journeys one sees his faith grow from a mere intellectual curiosity to a deep engagement with his own self, with the mysteries of God, and with the stories of people encountering that God in the Scriptures.

Feiler comes at his journeys as a Jew, but is intrigued by the differing understandings of Christians and Muslims concerning the same land, the same stories, the same religious figures. He discovers similar distortions in the three faiths as they each appropriate Abraham for themselves to the exclusion of others. But then Feiler also sees the same spiritual yearnings and lessons in the three faiths. He finds that life is defined by spirit and that we must leave what is comfortable, even our doctrinaire traditions, and go to unknown places at the call of God.

In his travels Feiler interviews scholars, clerics and ordinary people of all three Abrahamic faiths. Then after writing, *Abraham: A Journey to the Heart of Three Faiths*, Feiler devised a way to invite others to journey with him. He established the format for "Abraham Salons," gatherings of people of the three Abrahamic faiths to engage in guided discussions about Abraham and their own faiths. The Salons are a way for the participants to learn about each other, study the Biblical and Quranic passages together and build trust.

Early in *Abraham*, Feiler is introduced to a legendary story that is told by Jews, Christians and Muslims. The story speaks about how love between people is necessary before God can be manifest in the world. In a line that echoes themes from both Feiler's and Armstrong's work, a guide finally tells Feiler: "If you're not capable of living with each other and getting along with each other, then you're not capable of having a relationship with God. ... So the question is not whether God can bring peace into the world. The question is: Can we?"

❓ Discussion Questions
Chapters 16-24

Is there a story from another religious tradition that speaks with spiritual power to you? What in particular in that story gives the story its appeal and strength?

Some people who have learned from other religions have been accused of being syncretistic—blending components of two religions. Others seem to take a lesson from the teaching or practice found in another religion to heighten or strengthen their own faith understanding or practice. What do you think makes the difference between these two approaches? Where might adopting the thinking or practice of another religion be helpful and where might it be harmful? Or, perhaps in your experience, spiritual blending is welcomed and, if so, how do you decide what should be blended in this way?

Kabir, Evelyn Underhill, Simone Weil and many others have found mysticism as a key point for interfaith encounter and learning. Why do you think mysticism would be such a common bond for so many people of different religious traditions? Do you have any mystical aspects to your own spirituality? Does that mystical experience help you resonate with what you hear from people of other faiths? In what way?

Tolstoy, Gandhi, Khan, King, and Suu Kyi interacted and learned at the level of effective moral action in the political and social sphere. What is it about this area of interreligious encounter that opens up possibilities for learning? Have you found yourself working in common cause with people of different religions? What bound you together? Was there openness to a broader interfaith encounter or was your alliance only temporary and issue-centered?

E. Stanley Jones was willing to be challenged by persons of another faith in both his concepts and his practice. What does it take personally to be able to be challenged by another, to learn from that challenge, and to be strengthened rather than weakened in one's own faith?

In his book *Abraham*, Bruce Feiler recounts the comments of one of his guides: "If you're not capable of living with each other and getting along with each other, then you're not capable of having a relationship with God. ... So the question is not whether God can bring peace into the world. The question is: Can we?" What do you think of that question? Is bringing peace to the world God's challenge or ours? In what way? What might you do to respond to the challenge, both locally and globally?

Chapter 25

Religious Liberty
"The Golden Rule in Government Law"

Roger Williams Strauss was a Jewish leader in the early years of the National Conference for Christians and Jews (now known as the National Conference for Community and Justice, although both names often were shortened to NCCJ). His name is interesting, because this Jewish man was named after a Christian Baptist preacher!

Roger Williams

Roger Williams (featured in *Interfaith Heroes*) was the founder of the colony of Rhode Island. He had been banished from Massachusetts in 1635 under pain of death for preaching Baptist doctrines. So Williams traveled a bit south, purchased some land from the Narragansett tribe, and founded Rhode Island. Williams wrote religious liberty into the establishing documents of the colony. Rhode Island became a haven for Christian dissidents such as Quakers and Baptists. Jews also found haven there, establishing the second synagogue in America in Providence, Rhode Island. Because Jews found freedom in Rhode Island, the Baptist Roger Williams was held in such high regard that a Jewish family named their son after him. Religious liberty was treasured as a precious gift.

Religious liberty remains a hot issue. When U.S. President George W. Bush visited China during the Beijing Olympics he attended a church service to promote the cause of religious freedom in a country where Christians and Muslims are harassed by the government in some areas. Islamic countries that institute *Sharia* law find many Christians rising up in protest, and Bahá'ís in Iran have been severely persecuted. The Orthodox Christians in some post-Communist countries oppress minority Christian and Muslim groups. French schools ban Muslim girls from wearing the headscarf. Buddhists in South Korea take to the streets to protest religious bias from a Presbyterian President. Hindu militants affiliated with the ruling party in some Indian states attack Christian churches, homes and businesses and call for expelling all Muslims from India. Many societies struggle over whether to allow religious freedom, especially for minority groups, and how to define the limits of those freedoms.

Advocacy for religious freedom can be found deep in the annals of history. Perhaps the first known ruler to deal with religious diversity in a tolerant manner was the founder of the Persian Empire, Cyrus the Great (580-530 B.C.E.). After uniting the Medes and Persians, Cyrus conquered the Babylonian and Lydian empires and other kingdoms until his rule extended from the Indus River in the east to Asia Minor and Judea in the west. In an age when rulers were known for their brutality and might, Cyrus won people over through his generosity and acceptance of local customs. In particular he supported the various local religions throughout his realm, allowing people to worship their own gods and even to rebuild their ruined temples, which created much enthusiasm and support for his rule even from recently conquered peoples. One group so favored were the Jews who had been hauled off into captivity by the Babylonians following the destruction of Jerusalem. Once he had captured Babylon, Cyrus allowed the Jews who wished to return to Jerusalem to do so and to rebuild their temple. A Jewish prophet in Isaiah 45 praised Cyrus and called this pagan king the Lord's "anointed." In the "Cyrus Cylinder," a small clay cylinder with

Cyrus Cylinder

cuneiform writing, Cyrus presents himself as a beneficent king for allowing exiles to return home and take their gods with them. A replica of the "Cyrus Cylinder" is on display at the United Nations.

The Muslim Mughal ruler Akbar the Great (1542-1605, featured in *Interfaith Heroes*) promoted religious freedom in India. He created a period of internal stability in Indian society in large part through his support of religious freedom, abolishing taxes on certain religions, and promoting religious dialogue. In areas dominated by the Orthodox Christian Church in that same period Patriarch Metrophanes III (1520-1580) became an advocate for justice and peace toward people of other faiths. Following a report on attacks against Jews, the Patriarch wrote a landmark encyclical in which he said, "Injustice ... regardless to whomever acted upon or performed against, is still injustice. The unjust person is never relieved of the responsibility of these acts under the pretext that the injustice is done against a heterodox and not to a believer. As our Lord Jesus Christ in the Gospels said, do not oppress or accuse anyone falsely; do not make any distinction or give room to the believers to injure those of another belief." From a position of social and political dominance the Patriarch put the responsibility on those in power to prevent the unjust treatment of religious minorities.

Statue of Mary Dyer

In American history, the issue of religious liberty was first raised in the 1600s by dissidents in the Massachusetts Bay Colony where the Puritan Congregationalists controlled the state church and brooked no alternative expressions of faith. Mary Dyer, whose statue stands in Boston in front of the Massachusetts State House, was a Quaker woman who was hanged by the Puritan government. She spoke out for religious liberty and the freedom of conviction following the banning of a Quaker from her congregation. When offered clemency if she would recant, she responded, "What is life compared to the witness for Truth?" It was only a few years later that Roger Williams was driven out of Massachusetts and established Rhode Island.

When the 13 American colonies banded together to eventually become the United States, they had to deal with the question of religious difference. Some colonies were Anglican; some were Puritan. The religious liberty of Rhode Island and later Pennsylvania provided the example that eventually led to the Bill of Rights including religious freedom among the cherished values as the basis of our democracy. The newly elected President George Washington, himself a Deist, addressed a Jewish congregation in Newport, Rhode Island, in 1790 with these words: "The citizens of the United States of America have a right to applaud themselves for giving to mankind examples of an enlarged and liberal policy: a policy worthy of imitation. All possess alike liberty of conscience and immunities of citizenship. It is now no more that toleration is spoken of, as if it was by the indulgence of one class of people that another enjoyed the exercise of their inherent natural rights. For happily the Government of the United States, which gives to bigotry no sanction, to persecution no assistance, requires only that they who live under its protection, should demean themselves as good citizens, in giving it on all occasions their effectual support."

The principles of freedom laid out in the Bill of Rights and in Washington's statement were ideals often unmatched by the realities of community life in the United States. However, through the action of citizen advocates, active religious bodies, and judicial interpretations from the Supreme Court, religious liberty has been defined, refined and woven into the fabric of American life. Questions such as broadcasting the Muslim call to prayer, using peyote in Native American religious rites, Jehovah's Witnesses declining to say the Pledge of Allegiance in school, and the proper place of prayer in public school continue to challenge the American public and our courts to continue examining our religious liberty. Reflecting roots that go back to Rhode Island, the Baptist Joint Committee for Religious Liberty and the Jewish Public Affairs Committee often lead the way together toward religious liberty in the halls of Congress and the Supreme Court.

Chapter 26

Ashoka
(304-232 B.C.E.)

One must not exalt one's creed discrediting all others, nor must one degrade these others without legitimate reasons.

One must, on the contrary, render to other creeds the honor befitting them

Ashoka was the Indian emperor of the Maurya Dynasty whose religious conversion to Buddhism led to such a transformation that the one who used to be called "the cruel Ashoka" was called "the pious Ashoka." Through his transformed rule he earned the appellation "Ashoka the Great."

Born in 304 B.C.E., Ashoka rose to the thone in 273 B.C.E. He launched many military conquests, forging an empire that covered most of modern-day India and stretched even through Pakistan, Afghanistan and into Persia. In a war against Kalinga on the east coast of India his troops slaughtered over 100,000 people. Beholding the destruction the emperor lamented, "What have I done?" Haunted by the horrors he had perpetrated he began a spiritual quest that led him to convert to Buddhism. He abandoned war and violence and committed himself to an official policy of nonviolence or *ahimsa* (a term Mahatma Gandhi later utilized).

His policy, termed *Dharmashoka*, was based on a morality of nonviolence, truthfulness, mercy, egalitarianism and respect for all people. Even with neighboring empires Ashoka shifted his policy to one of respect, establishing good relations especially with the Hellenic societies to the west. He was an excellent administrator and a philanthropist. He established universities and instituted the protection of wildlife.

Ashoka was a strong promoter of the Buddhist religion, boosting the local religion in northern India into a world religion. He built thousands of *stupas* and monasteries for the Buddhist communities throughout his realm. He sent missionary monks to spread Buddhism in all directions. Ashoka's monks took Buddhism to Sri Lanka and Thailand, still major Buddhist countries to this day. He also claimed to have brought Buddhism to Greece and Egypt, but there is no record of this in the West, just the records of Ashoka himself. However, many Greeks who settled in India from the days of Alexander's conquests adopted Buddhism.

Though he was such a strong proponent of Buddhism, as a ruler Ashoka established policies of tolerance toward all religions. During his time India had Hindus, Jains, Ajivikas as well as Buddhists. Ashoka's edicts were inscribed on stone pillars throughout India, and his pillar at Sarnath with four lion heads at the top has become the symbol of today's Indian republic. Ashoka addressed religious tolerance directly and extensively in his edicts. He said, "All religions should reside everywhere, for all of them desire self-control and purity of heart." Another edict stated, "Contact (between religions) is good. One should listen to and respect the doctrines professed by others. Beloved-of-the-Gods, King Piyadasi (official titles of Ashoka) desires that all should be well-learned in the good doctrines of other religions." He inscribed, "One must not exalt one's creed discrediting all others, nor must one degrade these others without legitimate reasons. One must, on the contrary, render to other creeds the honor befitting them."

Ashoka the Great left a legacy of both religious fervor and religious tolerance. Holding a deep passion for one's own faith, particularly in his case a missionary faith, at the same time as encouraging the respect and learning about other religions was as unusual then as it is now.

CHAPTER 27

Abd-Ar-Rahman III and Al-Hakam II
(891-961)   (915-976)

During the reigns of Abd-ar-Rahman III and his son Al-Hakam II two "Golden Ages" occurred: The Golden Age of Arab rule in Iberia and The Golden Age of Jewish culture in Spain. During the half-century reign of Abd ar-Rahman (also sometimes written as Abd al-Rahman), Islamic Spain rose to its grandest and most prosperous era. He was the first of the Umayyad rulers of Spain to take the title of Caliph. He engaged in military activities both to secure the internal cohesion of his kingdom and to expand its borders against Christian enemies to the North and Muslim enemies in North Africa. By his death he had stabilized his realm and launched building projects that made Cordova one of the greatest cities in Europe.

Following the Arab Muslim conquest of Spain in the 8th Century, the repression of Jews by the Christian Visigoths was replaced by liberty to practice their religion under Moorish rule. As *dhimmis*, or "protected non-Muslims," Jews were only required to pay the *jizya* tax of one dinar per person. Payment of the *jizya* was separated from the administration of the Muslim *zakat* assessed for the poor. Jews were also exempt from military service. People of various religious beliefs were allowed the freedom to practice their religion, though public displays such as processions and bells were discouraged. The Jewish community prospered, becoming active in the economic life of Moorish Spain in a way that added to the economic strength of the whole society. The Jewish community was allowed to have its own legal system and social services. Adb ar-Rahman brought Jews into his court and into positions of social and academic leadership.

Though Al-Hakam II continued the policies of his father, including winning some major military victories, he was better known as a patron of the arts and sciences. Al-Hakam had a great love for scholarship and made Cordova a center of learning. He developed a library with more than 400,000 volumes. He expanded the university founded by his father by drawing not only Muslims, but also Christians, to its faculty and student body. Under Al-Hakam's sponsorship Jewish scholars translated many ancient Greek and Hebrew texts into Arabic. Jewish academics made major contributions in the fields of botany, geography, medicine, mathematics, poetry and philosophy.

The high-water mark of Moorish religious tolerance of Adb al-Rahman III and Al-Hakam II was followed by periods of increasing intolerance. First some of the books in the library established by Al-Hakam were viewed as heretical by the son who succeeded him and were burned. Then in 1011 and 1066 major pogroms against the Jews were launched by successive waves of puritanical Muslims. Jewish scholars who had flourished under Moorish tolerance and had made Cordova a center of learning left Spain for more moderate Muslim realms such as Morocco and Egypt. One such scholar was Moses Maimonides (featured in *Interfaith Heroes*) who eventually settled in Egypt.

Sometimes historical accuracy is difficult to discern because those telling the story have their own agendas that can distort or emphasize one point to the exclusion of other points. The current struggle over the story line of Moorish Spain is a case in point. The question of whether Muslims and non-Muslims can co-exist peacefully today is often argued with Moorish Spain as a debating point. Scholars still are trying to sort out whether the relationship between the dominant Moorish Muslim society was an exemplary model for interfaith relationships or whether it was just better than the religious intolerance exhibited during that period in Christian western Europe. Jews were allowed fewer rights than Muslims, but they were far better off especially during the days of Abd-ar-Rahman III and Al-Hakam II than in most of the Christian kingdoms at the time. Also adherents of Christian sects that were labeled "heretical" could find refuge and tolerance in Moorish Spain. Their more religiously tolerant rule created a place of economic, cultural and academic vitality.

Chapter 28

King John Sigismund and Isabella Jagiello
(1540-1571) (1519-1559)

Each person [should] maintain whatever religious faith he wishes, with old or new rituals, while we at the same time leave it to their judgment to do as they please in the matter of faith, just so long as they bring no harm to bear on anyone at all.

Transylvania has had its name unfortunately linked with the vampire Dracula, based on Bram Stoker's horror novel. It is debatable whether Stoker's vampire had any inspirational roots with Count Vlad III Dracula, also known as Vlad the Impaler, beyond the name and evil reputation. But Transylvania has a nobler heritage that needs to be brought to fresh light to inspire the contemporary world as we deal with matters of religious differences in our various nations.

In the 1500s Transylvania stood on the conflicted borders of two major cultures with different religions. In much of Europe, Christianity was in turmoil. The dominant Roman Catholic Church had been shaken by the Protestant Reformation, which led to the creation of the Lutheran Churches and the Reformed Churches (Calvinists) as well as many other smaller religious movements. To the south was the Ottoman Empire, still growing in strength under the dynamic leadership of Sultan Suleiman the Magnificent. These conflicts and moving lines of control passed over Transylvania, and in their wake a very diverse population developed. In Transylvania one could find Roman Catholics, Romanian Orthodox, Lutherans, Calvinists, Unitarians, Jews and perhaps even a few Muslims.

Into this roiling brew of social, political and religious ferment a young Polish woman named Isabella Jagiellon was married to a claimant to the Hungarian throne. After her husband died, Isabella continued on as a widow queen. When Suleiman the Magnificent swept through the region, he set up Isabella as queen to rule with her young son over Transylvania. Eventually the region was handed over to Austria in a treaty, and the Austro-Hungarian authorities retained her in Transylvania.

Queen Isabella's personal physician was an early Unitarian, Giorgio Biandrata. This religious refugee from Italy taught her about religious tolerance. Convinced by his teachings, Isabella issued the "Decree of Religious Tolerance" in 1557. The decree called for "each person to maintain whatever religious faith he wishes, with old or new rituals, while We at the same time leave it to their judgment to do as they please in the matter of faith, just so long as they bring no harm to bear on anyone at all." During a period of interreligious relationships expressed through war, inquisition and burning at the stake, this was a remarkable document.

Isabella died shortly after promulgating the "Decree of Religious Tolerance." Her son John II Sigismund Zápolya, still a teenager, assumed the throne. During his reign he strengthened the work of religious tolerance that his mother began, continuing to employ Dr. Biandrata as his advisor. King John Sigismund had a strong interest in religion, but not just for his own beliefs at the expense of the religions of his subjects. Instead he encouraged open discussions about religion and a toleration and respect for all viewpoints. He even sponsored a great 10-day public debate with Lutherans, Calvinists, Catholics and Unitarians, at the end of which he announced his personal embrace of Unitarianism. He believed these issues could be discussed without recourse to war or repression.

John Sigismund renewed the decree his mother had passed, but five years later he took it back to the Transylvanian Diet asking that it be strengthened. The result was the Act of Religious Tolerance and Freedom of Conscience, also known as the Edict of Torda, the broadest expression of religious freedom in Europe to that point in history. The Act, passed in 1568, encouraged preachers to preach in the way that their souls compelled them, and said that congregations could keep preachers whose teachings they approved. The Act said, "No one shall be reviled for his religion by anyone, according to the previous statutes, and it is not permitted that anyone should threaten anyone else by imprisonment or by removal from his post for his teaching, for faith is the gift of God."

Through these policies of religious tolerance King John Sigismund, following in the footsteps of his mother Queen Isabella Jagiello, made Transylvania the freest kingdom in terms of religion in all of Europe. King John died in a carriage accident, and eight years after the Edict of Torda was passed it was overturned by the next king. Regrettably Transylvania slid away from the spirit of tolerance that had flourished under John Sigismund into the religious conflict and repression that plagued surrounding regions.

Chapter 29

Haym Salomon
(1740-1785)

The U.S. Postal Service called Haym Salomon "Financial Hero of the American Revolution" when a commemorative stamp was issued hailing his contribution. He was born in Poland, and after extensive travels arrived in New York in 1772. He quickly became a successful merchant and dealer in foreign securities. He got involved in the Sons of Liberty in New York. When war broke out he used his wealth to supply the American troops.

When the British occupied New York City, Salomon was arrested and imprisoned. Because he was multilingual, thanks to his early life in Europe, the British employed him to aid in communication with their Hessian mercenaries. Taking advantage of access he gained as translator, Salomon covertly helped prisoners of the British escape. When he was caught urging the German Hessians to desert the British cause, he was promptly re-arrested. His property was confiscated, and he was sentenced to hang. Assisted by the Sons of Liberty,

Haym Salomon escaped from the British and fled to Philadelphia.

In Philadelphia, though he began penniless, he resumed his brokerage business. The French, who had allied with the American colonial army, employed him as their paymaster. He helped secure loans from the Dutch and Spanish governments for the struggling Continental Congress, eventually helping the fledgling nation get onto a sound financial footing. He also provided personal interest-free loans to many of the leaders in the Continental Congress, so that they were free to pursue leadership in the revolutionary struggle.

Throughout his career in the patriotic cause he fought against the prejudices and stereotypes of Jewish financiers as profiteers. His personal honesty and integrity was so well known that his mere signature could act as a sufficient guarantee. He would back up all commitments even at personal cost to himself if need be. Salomon died with more debts than assets because he gave so much for the birth of his country, many of his debts coming from the purchase of government debt. He passionately and directly countered those negative stereotypes of Jews, sometimes bringing criticism upon himself, but he never surrendered his ideals. Though his descendents in the 19th Century tried to obtain compensation from the U.S. Government, none was ever forthcoming because all documentation had disappeared or was in depreciated continental currency.

Haym Salomon provided leadership in the Jewish community both in Philadelphia, where he was on the governing council of Congregation Mikveh Israel, and for the national Jewish community. He personally contributed a quarter of the cost for building the Mikveh Israel synagogue. He used his wealth as a philanthropist, becoming treasurer for the Philadelphia society to assist indigent travelers passing through the region. He based his assistance on a person's need and his own ideals of liberty and freedom for all people.

As the new government was taking shape, Salomon fought against laws that prohibited non-Christians from serving in public office, successfully leading the fight to repeal the test oath in Pennsylvania. He was a pioneer in establishing religious liberty for all people as one of the foundations for the United States.

In 1975 the United States Postal Service issued a stamp commemorating Haym Salomon's contribution to the U.S. Revolution.

Salomon often preferred to remain in the background, so the exact role he played seldom came into the public light. As a result many legends developed around him, and historical verification of some of the stories has sometimes been difficult. Poor documentation of the financial records of that time also makes accurate accounts impossible. However, there can be no denying that at key points in the Revolution and then in the development of the young United States, Haym Salomon played a pivotal role in enabling the movement to go forward.

Chapter 30

John Leland
(1754-1841)

*The liberty I contend for is more than toleration.
The very idea of toleration is despicable; it supposes
that some have a pre-eminence above the rest to grant
indulgence, whereas all should be equally free.*

A Baptist preacher who knew how to play political hardball ensured that freedom of religion was inscribed into the United States Constitution. The author of that founding document, who would later become President of the United States, is well known: James Madison. But the preacher who challenged Madison on religious liberty is an interfaith hero known only in a few circles today.

John Leland joined the Baptists as a young man, quickly became a preacher, and left his native Massachusetts for Virginia. The time was 1776, just as the American War of Independence was getting underway. After winning their revolution, the struggling colonies tried to organize together under the *Articles of Confederation*, but that document proved inadequate to hold them together effectively. A Constitutional Convention was convened in Philadelphia to draft a new document, which was primarily penned by James Madison. The U.S. Constitution was completed on

September 17, 1787, and sent to the individual former colonies for ratification.

That is when John Leland stepped into the process. Besides engaging in his revivalist preaching, Leland spoke and wrote extensively on the topic of religious liberty. He wrote: "Government should protect every man in thinking and speaking freely, and see that one does not abuse another. The liberty I contend for is more than toleration. The very idea of toleration is despicable; it supposes that some have a pre-eminence above the rest to grant indulgence, whereas all should be equally free, Jews, Turks, Pagans and Christians." All of the states except for Rhode Island and Pennsylvania had official state churches. Leland mobilized the Baptists in Virginia to push for religious liberty in Virginia. The Baptists were almost the only group to support Thomas Jefferson's "Act for Establishing Religious Freedom" as opposed to Patrick Henry's bill to assess taxes to support "teachers of the Christian religion." James Madison joined the cause, and Madison's version of the bill eventually passed in the Virginia General Assembly.

Leland urged Madison to press the issue further into the U.S. Constitution, perhaps adding on a "Bill of Rights" as an amendment. Madison initially opposed the idea of an amendment. So Leland ran against Madison as a delegate to Virginia's convention to ratify the constitution. With the support of Baptists throughout the state it became clear that Leland had more votes that Madison. Madison visited Leland's farm and they thrashed out an agreement. Leland would withdraw from the race for the convention, and Madison would join Leland in calling for an amendment to the Constitution guaranteeing religious liberty, free speech and a free press. On June 7, 1789, Madison submitted the first version what became the First Amendment to the Bill of Rights. Religious freedom was enshrined in U.S. law.

Getting the concept of religious liberty in the Bill of Rights was just the first step. How would those legal words be interpreted? Leland continued speaking and writing on the topic. Using the pen name of Jack Nipps, he wrote articles in *The Yankee Spy* published in Boston, developing an extensive political philosophy on the relationship between religion and the state. He wrote that "it is not possible in the nature of things to establish religion by human laws without perverting the design of civil law and oppressing the people." Leland spoke in strong defense of those whose beliefs were different from his own: "Is it the duty of a deist to support that which he believes to be a cheat and imposition? Is it the duty of the Jew to support the religion of Jesus Christ, when he really believes that he was an imposter? Must the papist be forced to pay men for preaching down the supremacy of the pope, whom they are sure is the head of the church? Government has no more to do with the religious opinions of men than it has to do with the principles of mathematics."

Baptist concepts of religious liberty and freedom of conscience were forged from the persecutions they endured at the hands of the state churches and governments in England and Massachusetts. The early Baptists realized that for anyone to have their religious rights genuinely protected, all must be protected, including and especially religious minorities. So these interfaith heroes, led by Roger Williams and later John Leland, did the groundbreaking political work that pushed into the founding documents of the United States the religious freedom that protects everyone of every religion.

? Discussion Questions
Chapters 25-30

What are some of the issues related to religion and government that you have seen recently in the news or heard about in your local community? What do you think about these issues? Do the examples or teachings of any of the interfaith heroes in this section speak to how those issues might best be resolved?

What does religious freedom mean to you? Should there be any limits set on the freedom of religion? How should the rights of religious minorities be protected? Have you ever felt that your religious rights were restricted? In what way? Should the government have done anything about the situation?

Some religious people view their practice of their faith as a totally private affair. Others hold that religion involves a person's deeply held values, which by nature are acted out in life, including in the social and political sphere. What do you think about the place of religious values? Should religion shape social and political debates? What is an appropriate use of religious values in trying to find public agreement on various issues? When do religious beliefs become a problem in the public sphere?

John Leland said, "Government has no more to do with the religious opinions of men than it has to do with the principles of mathematics." Do you agree or disagree? Why?

Leland believed that government intervention in support of the practice of religion actually undermined the vitality of religion itself. Do you agree? In what ways might Leland be right? In what ways might government play a constructive role related to religion and religious practice? In what ways might government action related to religion undercut the power and status of religious faith?

The word "toleration" has sometimes been used as a positive word and other times been viewed as paternalistic and elitist. How do you understand "religious tolerance"? What is good about tolerance? What is problematic?

Chapter 31

Providing Refuge
How Far Will Love Go?

One of the most cogent critics of Iranian President Mahmoud Ahmadinejad's belittling of the Holocaust is a Muslim in the U.S. Ma'sood Cajee, a member of the Muslim Peace Fellowship, wrote an article for the Fellowship of Reconciliation in which he critiqued the anti-Holocaust rhetoric that reached a peak in the controversial conference in Iran orchestrated to debunk the Holocaust "myth." Cajee makes his case from the Islamic scriptures and traditions that warn against mocking and ridiculing what others hold sacred. He points to the harm done to the status and credibility of Muslims everywhere by Ahmadinejad's statements. But one of Cajee's most telling points is that this anti-Holocaust rhetoric destroys the stories of Muslim heroes who were part of the resistance to the Nazi program of exterminating Jews. There are many stories about Muslims in Albania, France, Bosnia-Herzegovina, Turkey and Tunisia who hid Jews and helped them escape to safe haven. These Muslims put their lives at risk, and sometimes lost their lives, to help their Jewish neighbors. Because of contemporary politics related to Israel in the Middle East some Muslims have been trying to rewrite history and minimize or even deny the Holocaust. In the process, however, they are losing the stories of courageous people of their own faith who in their context did what was moral and right and shone as bright lights in a desolate period of history.

World War II was the most widespread and violent conflict in human history. In the middle of the war in Europe was the Nazi program to exterminate those they considered "undesirable," with Jews as the central target of the Nazi Final Solution. The sheer scope of the Holocaust provided many opportunities for rescue of Jews by Christians and Muslims and also provided a backdrop of horror that starkly highlights the heroism of the rescuers. Some of these stories are featured in *Interfaith Heroes*, namely the stories of the Albanian Muslims and André Trocmé, and more stories from this era are featured in this section of this volume. Many other stories of heroic rescuers during the Holocaust are told elsewhere, most notably at the Yad Vashem Holocaust Memorial in Israel. Yad Vashem recognizes such heroes as "The Righteous Among the Nations," naming people whose courageous deeds have been authenticated and preserving as detailed a history as possible.

Providing shelter to people in need has often been a highly valued religious act. The Jewish, Christian and Sikh houses of worship have often been associated with "sanctuary" not just for worshipers but for people fleeing threats or destitution. The Hebrew Scriptures in Numbers established six cities of refuge to which people could flee for safety if they had committed accidental manslaughter. In a related Jewish tradition the horns of the altar became a safe place to which people could flee. The Greeks and Romans developed similar places. Romulus, the mythical founder of Rome, was said to have established the Palatine Hill as a place where fugitives could seek refuge. He erected a temple to Asylæus where these fugitives could come, thus providing the linguistic roots for our contemporary English word "asylum."

Christians in Europe set up sanctuary towns or churches. The Theodosian Code in 392 C.E. is the first known Christian legal record of such practices. The Code provided for fugitives to find sanctuary on all church grounds, but not within the walls of the churches themselves. The Theodosian Code was not noted for its interfaith value, however, for it explicitly excluded public debtors, Jews, heretics and apostates from refuge.

For Sikhs the *gurdwara* was not only the place for worship but also a community center and place of shelter for the homeless and others in special need. In Canada in the early 1900s a Sikh temple became a focal point for immigrants trying to slip into Canada, providing a beacon when the border with the U.S. was safe to cross. A hundred years later another Sikh temple provided sanctuary for asylum seekers fleeing deportation by Canadian authorities.

During the 1980s many congregations in the United States provided sanctuary for refugees from El Salvador and Guatemala. Though the refugees were fleeing the violence of military dictatorships and their death squads, the U.S. government would not provide asylum because the U.S. was supporting the regimes in those two countries. Asylum seekers from Nicaragua, whose government was opposed by the U.S., were welcomed, but those from El Salvador and Guatemala risked being returned to face possible torture and death. So churches and synagogues participated in the "Sanctuary Movement" that both sheltered asylum-seekers in their buildings and smuggled people through the U.S. to Canada. Some church leaders were arrested and jailed for their activities. The Sanctuary Movement for Central Americans drew inspiration from the Underground Railroad movement that helped bring thousands of escaped slaves from the American South to freedom in Canada in the years before emancipation. Years earlier some congregations had also provided sanctuary to draft resisters during the Vietnam War.

At the beginning of the 21st Century a "New Sanctuary Movement" has been launched to support illegal immigrants in the face of imminent deportation because of what is viewed as harsh or unjust legislation. The U.S. Congress was considering legislation to criminalize providing humanitarian aid to people without first checking on their legal status. Cardinal Roger Mahony of the Archdiocese of Los Angeles instructed all his priests and staff to disregard the law if it passed. The proposed legislation and Cardinal Mahony's resistance sparked the formation of the New Sanctuary Movement in 2007 with people from a wide range of Christian denominations, Jews, Muslims and Sikhs participating in the organizing meeting. Besides providing sanctuary for families facing deportation, the movement encourages advocacy for legislation that would prevent officials from breaking up families and that would bring about comprehensive and just immigration reform.

When there are religious differences between the refugee and the rescuer, then interfaith dimensions of providing shelter come into consideration. The Christian Abyssian King Negus provided refuge for followers of Muhammad in the early 600s, though opponents tried to get him to deny such refuge for people of a different faith. Throughout history, various political regimes proclaimed religious freedom and established refuges for religious fugitives. Such regimes included Moorish Spain under Abd-ar-Rahman III and Al-Hakam II and the Rhode Island colony established by Roger Williams. Furthermore, when the rescuer is acting in contradiction to the policies and actions of the dominant society, then the risk to the rescuer may be increased. Often, however, that risk-taking is centered in the rescuer's own religious commitments.

Rescue becomes truly heroic when the one providing refuge is physically endangered as well and can suffer from violence along with the fugitive. Such was the case for rescuers during the Holocaust. Such bravery continues to this day. During the ethnic and religious violence in Indonesia following the collapse of Suharto's government, many Christians were attacked by militant Muslims and their churches vandalized or destroyed. Yet there were many cases of Muslim families hiding their Christian neighbors from the marauding gangs in the streets. Similar actions took place in the violence by Hindu extremist groups against Christians in India during 2007 and 2008. While churches were being burned along with Christian homes and businesses, Christians told stories of some Hindu neighbors who hid them or in some cases stood between them and their attackers even to the point of suffering severe beatings. While this section provides stories out of the Holocaust, there are many stories waiting to be found and waiting to be told from many places of sorrow where people acted courageously to provide refuge across lines of religious difference.

 The Jewish Torah teaches that whoever saves a person saves the whole world in turn. "Saving the world" or "saving humanity" is so vast as to be meaningless. But saving the person in desperate straights standing in front of us is a concrete challenge to our moral and religious life. May we have the courage to act as these interfaith heroes did when our moment of choice comes.

Chapter 32

Irena Sendler
(1910-2008)

Every child saved with my help is the justification of my existence on this Earth, and not a title to glory.

The identities of 2,500 Jewish children were hidden in a bottle buried in a back yard by the Polish Catholic woman who helped rescue them from certain death. The identity of this interfaith hero was also buried under the weight of Communist rule and condemnation for her activities. When the story emerged to the wider public, thanks to four U.S. school children, a humble hero was recognized and acclaimed.

Irena Sendler was born in Otwock, Poland, where her father was a doctor. He died in 1917 caring for poor Jewish people during a typhus epidemic, but passed on to her a sense of solidarity and care that crossed religious and ethnic lines. As a student Sendler was dismissed from Warsaw University for failing to comply with Jewish segregation laws. When the Germans invaded Poland, Irena immediately began to help Jews by delivering food and other supplies to them. She was a social worker with the Contagious Disease Department, where some of the staff was connected to Zegota, the Polish resistance. She registered Jewish families with fictitious Christian names, labeled their homes as infected with typhus or tuberculosis to prevent German inspections, then brought meals and social services to the families.

In 1942, the Nazis herded all the Warsaw Jews into a sealed off district that became known as the Warsaw Ghetto. In a 16-block area of the city, a new wall imprisoned 450,000 Jews. Many people died of hunger and disease before the Nazis starting shipping Jews to the Treblinka death camp. Irena was chosen to head up the Zegota's children's department. As a social worker she gained access to the Ghetto where she would don a Star of David armband in solidarity with the suffering Jews inside. Along with her staff of 24 women and one man she began to smuggle Jewish children out of the ghetto as well as care for children who had escaped the ghetto by other means. She and her staff hid children under stretchers in her ambulance, helped them get out through sewer pipes, or carried them out in trunks or sacks. Desperate parents would ask, "Can you guarantee they will live?" Sendler could only guarantee they would die if they stayed. She later said, "In my dreams I still hear the cries when they left their parents."

Sendler carefully noted the names and family identities of each child and where they were placed so that after the war the children would know who they were and could be reunited with any surviving parents. The children were hidden with nuns and priests and placed in Catholic orphanages. She issued thousands of forged documents to protect the children. Eventually she and her staff helped 2,500 children escape. Knowing she was being watched and was at risk, Sendler kept the list of names on thin tissue paper in two bottles buried under an apple tree in her neighbor's yard.

In October 1943 Irena Sendler was arrested by the Gestapo. They put her in the notorious Pawiak Prison where she was interrogated and tortured. The bones in her legs and feet were broken, leaving her crippled for life, but she refused to divulge any information about the children or her associates. Her execution was ordered, but the Zegota bribed the executioner who dumped her battered body in the forest and then wrote public announcements about her death. She escaped with the Zegota and continued her resistance activities until the end of the war.

Immediately after the war ended, Sendler unearthed the bottles and began the quest to find the rescued Jewish children and reunite them with their families. However, most of the parents and relatives had perished in either the ghetto or Treblinka. The children had only known her by her code name "Jolanta," but years later when her picture was published in a newspaper she got many calls from people who said, "I remember your face; it was you who took me out of the ghetto!"

When the Communists took over Poland at the end of World War II, Sendler was branded a fascist for her underground activities, and her story was suppressed. Though she was recognized by Israel's Yad Vashem Memorial as one of the "Righteous Among the Nations," few knew about her. Only when Communism fell in Poland did the word get out about the wartime heroism of this now elderly woman. In 1999 a teacher at a school in Uniontown, Kansas, encouraged four students to investigate the life of Irena Sendler, beginning with a snippet about Sendler in *U.S. News and World Report* in 1994. Those students, Megan Stewart, Elizabeth Cambers, Jessica Shelton and Sabrina Coons, began to research the story behind the sentence that had appeared in the news magazine. They then wrote a play based on their research titled *Life in a Jar*, a reference to the hiding place for the list of children's names. Their play was performed hundreds of times in Kansas, then across the U.S. and in Europe, and many other students have gotten involved in the play and project.

Eventually the children met Irena Sendler, frail and in her 90s, and cared for by Elzbieta Ficowska, a Jewish woman rescued by Sendler when she was 5 months old. They returned to Poland five times, learning more of the story first-hand. They established a website about Irena Sendler that has drawn millions of readers. Through the play and the website, the story of the life and courage of Irena Sendler, which was suppressed for so long, has become an inspiration around the world. Michael Glowinski, one of the child survivors, told the *Life in a Jar* students, "You have rescued the story of the rescuer."

Megan Stewart plays Irena Sendler in Life in a Jar

Irena Sendler received many honors for her actions, but she never claimed credit. She said, "I could have done more. This regret will follow me to my death." She also wrote in a letter that Ms. Ficowska read to the Polish Parliament when Sendler has honored by the Government of Poland for her actions, "Every child saved with my help is the justification of my existence on this Earth, and not a title to glory. Over a half-century has passed since the hell of the Holocaust, but its specter still hangs over the world and doesn't allow us to forget."

Chapter 33

Titus Brandsma
(1881-1942)

Do not yield to hatred. Be patient. We are here in a dark tunnel but we have to go on

Titus Brandsma, born in 1881 and named Anno Sjoerd, was a Dutch Carmelite priest who also worked as a university professor and a journalist. When he joined the Carmelites in 1898 he took a new name according to Carmelite tradition, Titus, his father's name and the name of the author of a New Testament epistle. He was a founder of the Catholic University of Nijmegan, now Radboud University, where he taught philosophy and the history of mysticism. His studies in mysticism centered on St. Teresa of Avila, whose works he had translated into Dutch.

In 1935 Brandsma also was appointed as spiritual advisor to the 30 Catholic newspapers in Holland, the context in which his final great work was to be done. As the Nazi ideology began to rise in Germany Brandsma became a critic of both the Nazi oppression of the Jews and the Nazi threats to freedom of the press. He issued strong public statements as early as 1935. "The Nazi movement is a black lie," he proclaimed. "It is pagan." Even before the war broke out his critiques made him a marked man for Dutch fascists.

When Germany invaded Holland in May, 1940, and Jewish students were ordered expelled from all the universities, he personally protested to the authorities. Brandsma drafted a pastoral letter that was issued by the Dutch Catholic bishops to be read in all the Catholic churches in Holland. The pastoral letter said that Nazism was incompatible with Catholic teaching at its very core. It condemned the anti-Semitic measures of the Nazis and decried the first deportation of Dutch Jews. The Catholic sacraments were refused to Nazi sympathizers because National Socialism was viewed to seriously corrupt the Christian conception of life for all who participated in it.

Then Brandsma wove together his criticisms of the oppression of the Jews and the denial of press freedom in a defiant action against the Nazi occupation government. All newspapers had been ordered to run Nazi propaganda against the Jews as well as the various edicts. As spiritual advisor to the Catholic press Brandsma traveled throughout Holland to meet with each Catholic editor to urge their resistance to this order. He knew the risks of such defiance, but he was determined to act in accordance with his conscience. He made it halfway through the circuit of editors when he was arrested by the Gestapo at the Boxmeer Monastery where years earlier he had begun his novitiate. Gestapo Captain Hardegen who interrogated him later explained that Brandsma was basically "an enemy of the German mission" and that "his hostility is proved by his writing against German policy toward the Jews."

Father Brandsma was sent to various Gestapo prisons before finally ending up in the Dachau concentration camp. Though he was sickly at his arrest, he was brutally treated at Dachau. Witnesses in the prisons and camp spoke of his prayerfulness and how he refused to become bitter. They also spoke about his pastoral care toward his fellow inmates, both Christians and Jews. His pastoral services often drew violent responses when they were noticed by the guards. Following severe beatings with clubs, Brandsma exhorted his fellow prisoners: "Do not yield to hatred. Be patient. We are here in a dark tunnel but we have to go on. At the end, the eternal light is shining for us." In Dachau as his health continued to deteriorate he was put into the sadistic medical experimentation program. The Nazi doctors injected him with a lethal dose of acid. His body was burned in the crematorium. Titus Brandsma was the first victim of the Nazis to be officially declared a martyr, and in 1985 he was beatified by Pope John Paul II.

CHAPTER 34

Si Kaddour Ben Ghabrit
(1868-1954)

Their children are like our own children. The one who encounters one of his children must give that child shelter and protection for as long as misfortune—or sorrow—lasts.

Amid the contemporary controversies in the Middle East, some stories of Muslims providing shelter to Jews have been forgotten or overlooked. Perhaps the telling and reclaiming of such stories can support new perspectives across lines of ethnic and religious difference, opening possibilities for reconciliation.

One such story involves the heroic efforts of the imam and congregation of the Grande Mosque de Paris during the Nazi occupation of France in World War II. Imam Si Kaddour ben Ghabrit led a mosque-based resistance effort that provided shelter and travel assistance to as many as 1,700 French Jews.

When the German army conquered France, the Grande Mosque de Paris first sheltered resistance fighters and North Africans who had escaped from German POW camps. The

Algerian immigrants in the mosque were mostly Berbers, mostly from the Kabylia region. They used their Berber Tamazight dialect to communicate, which made their resistance cells virtually impossible to infiltrate. At the heart of the mosque's resistance work was ben Ghabrit. Ben Ghabrit had three nationalities—Algerian, Moroccan and French—which allowed him to slip in and out of many contexts.

On July 16, 1942, the French Vichy government ordered the Paris police to round up the 28,000 Jews listed on the census the Germans had ordered. Because some police officers leaked word of the sweep only 13,000 Jews, including 4,000 children were seized. Ben Ghabrit produced a tract in Tamazight that was read aloud throughout the immigrant hostels in Paris: "Yesterday at dawn, the Jews of Paris were arrested. The old, the women, and the children. In exile like ourselves, workers like ourselves. They are our brothers. Their children are like our own children. The one who encounters one of his children must give that child shelter and protection for as long as misfortune—or sorrow—lasts." The Jews captured in the July police raids were shipped off to Auschwitz. Around 1,700 Jews who evaded capture were provided short-term shelter either in the mosque itself or in apartments nearby. Ben Ghabrit set up an alternate system that allowed the Jewish fugitives to hide if the Germans or French police came to the mosque, even if necessary going to the women's prayer room where men were not admitted. The imam wrote many false birth certificates and other forged documents to hide Jewish children under Muslim identities.

After providing initial sanctuary, the members of the mosque helped smuggle the Jews out to safety in Algeria or Spain. Some slipped out through the sewers directly underneath the mosque. Others were able to get out on wine barges down the Seine, hiding in barrels as Kabyl men steered the barges south.

Ben Ghabrit was viewed with suspicion by the German Gestapo. He was brought in for interrogation and threatened, but because the Nazis hoped to gain the support of France's Arab subjects they never did arrest this community leader.

Now as new conflicts stir up hatreds to erase the heroism of people like Si Kaddour ben Ghabrit from memory, perhaps the line from his tract can be an inspiration to call us all to our deeper human oneness and courageous compassion in the face of hatred and violence: "Their children are like our own children."

CHAPTER 35

Dervis Korkut
(d. 1969)

The wise Preacher in the Hebrew Scriptures said, "Cast your bread upon the waters, for you will find it after many days" (Ecclesiastes 11.1). This ancient word was made fresh in a modern story of rescue that came to an amazing full circle.

Dervis Korkut was curator of books and manuscripts at the Sarajevo Museum. He was from a prominent Bosnian Muslim family of liberal intellectuals. He studied theology in Istanbul and Paris. When Nazis occupied Yugoslavia during World War II Korkut spoke out about the anti-Semitic policies of the occupation. Korkut had worked very closely with the Jewish community as a scholar translating old documents. In the 1920s he had defended the Jewish community against anti-Jewish laws. Then when the Nazis took over he sent a position paper to the occupation government titled "Anti-Semitism Is Foreign to the Muslims of Bosnia and Herzegovina." He wrote that anti-Semitism was "only the lightning rod used to draw the people's attention away from their real problems." He presented the vision of pluralism in Bosnia: "The most beautiful proof of religious tolerance in Bosnia is that (in Sarajevo) all four domestic religious houses of worship (Catholic, Orthodox, Muslim and Jewish) were exactly one beside the other." Then Korkut was introduced to Mira Papo, and his resistance to the Nazi policies became personal.

Mira Papo came from a Jewish family that had fled the Spanish Inquisition in 1492, finally settling in Sarajevo. In 1941 the Nazis arrested the Jewish men in Sarajevo, including her father Salomon Papo, and shipped them off to the concentration camps. Then the women were ordered to gather together, but Mira refused. Her mother convinced her to resist, and the nineteen-year old watched her family members loaded onto trucks, never to be seen again. Of the 75,000 Jews in Yugoslavia before the war only 12,000 survived.

Papo then joined the Yugoslav Communist partisans fighting the Nazis. In 1942 the partisans took away the weapons of the Jewish members and sent the Jewish partisans unarmed to Sarajevo. Most of the Jews were caught and killed, but Papo found her way to the front of the finance ministry building where her father had once worked. A man came up to her and said, "Aren't you the daughter of Salomon Papo?" It was a porter who had once worked with her father. He walked with her to the Sarajevo Museum and introduced her to Dervis Korkut.

Korkut and his wife Servet took Papo into their home. They had a baby boy named Munib, so they developed the story that Papo was a Muslim woman hired to tend to the baby. Papo wore the full robes of traditional Muslim dress and went by the Muslim name of Amira. For four months Papo never left the Korkut home, and whenever German officers looked in they never expressed suspicions about the "servant" in traditional garb. In August 1942 false documents were procured and arrangements made to smuggle Papo to a safe area on the Dalmatian coast of Yugoslavia where she spent the rest of the war.

Genocide may be about more than killing people. It can also be about destroying the culture and memory of a people. Korkut saved one Jewish woman, but he also saved a Jewish cultural masterpiece, the Sarajevo *Haggadah*. The *Haggadah* is an illustrated Passover text used during the traditional Jewish

Passover Seder. The Sarajevo *Haggadah* is the oldest Sephardic *Haggadah* in the world and is considered to also be the most beautiful. Produced on 109 pages of bleached calfskin, the Sarajevo *Haggadah* has wine stains on some of the pages, showing that was used at many Seders in Jewish homes. It had been brought from Spain to Bosnia where it was sold to the museum in 1894.

Page from the Sarajevo Haggadah

In 1942 a Nazi general burst into the Sarajevo Museum looking to steal Jewish treasures for himself and demanded that the director give him the *Haggadah*. The director said he had given the document to a German lieutenant a few hours earlier who claimed to have come from the general. The general demanded the name of the lieutenant, but the director said he had no right to ask the name of a German officer. While the director was holding the general at bay with this false story, Dervis Korkut slipped out the back door of the museum with the *Haggadah*. He traveled deep into the Bosnian hills to the farm of a Muslim friend. There the priceless manuscript was hidden for the duration of the war, and according to some reports was kept for a while under the floorboards of a small rural mosque.

After the war Korkut was imprisoned by the new Communist government under false charges he had participated with a Muslim fascist militia. The testimony of Jewish friends saved him from the firing squad, but he spent six years in prison. After his release a daughter named Lamija was born to Dervis and Servet. In 1969 Dervis Korkut died. His daughter met an Albanian Muslim man named Vllaznim Jaha. They were married and lived in Pristina, Kosovo. Meanwhile, Mira Papo had settled in Israel, where in 1994 her testimony about her rescue by Dervis and Servet Korkut finally led to recognition of this brave couple. They were honored with the "Medal of the Righteous Among the Nations" and their names engraved on the Honour Wall in the Garden of the Righteous at the Yad Vashem Holocaust Memorial. Lamija Jaha was given a certificate about her parents' honor.

Then war broke out between Serbs and Albanians in Kosovo. The Serb army and militia engaged in "ethnic cleansing" against the Albanians in Kosovo, and the Jaha family fled with thousands of other refugees into Macedonia. While in the refugee camps Lamija tried to find a nation that would take them in, but even European countries where she had relatives would not provide them sanctuary. In the chaos of their flight from Kosovo Lamija had grabbed the certificate from Yad Vashem. One official who saw it suggested that she contact Israeli officials. When she presented the document to Israeli officials her entire family was brought to Israel for temporary shelter. Lamija and her family were warmly met at the airport by the son of Mira Papo. Eventually this Muslim refugee family from Kosovo became citizens of Israel, finding welcome for having sheltered a Jew during an earlier time of "ethnic cleansing."

Chapter 36

Corrie Ten Boom
(1892-1983)

You say we could lose our lives for this child.
I would consider that the greatest honor that could come to
my family.

During World War II a 50-year old single woman had a brick wall built through her bedroom to create a "hiding place" for Jews and other fugitives from the Nazis who had occupied her country. Corrie ten Boom and her family suffered and some of them died in providing shelter during the genocidal storm that swept Europe.

The ten Booms lived in Haarlem, Holland, where Corrie came from a long line of watchmakers. She learned the trade and became the first woman licensed in Holland as a watchmaker. She also engaged in social work, organizing girls clubs and also groups for families with developmentally disabled children.

Then in 1940 the German army invaded and occupied Holland. The Nazis banned Corrie's girls clubs, but the heaviest restrictions fell upon the Jews of Holland. As Jews started to be arrested and their property seized, the ten Boom family joined the Dutch underground in assisting Jews to escape. At first they kept small numbers of fugitives for a night or two before helping them make their way to other safe houses and eventually to neutral countries or to remote places where they could hide throughout the war. Corrie helped secure a hundred precious food ration cards that were only supposed to be given to non-Jews. Corrie took the illegally gained ration cards and distributed them to help feed the Jews in hiding. When the ten Booms were sheltering a family with a baby a friend who was a pastor of a church in a village outside Haarlem visited them. They asked if the pastor would take the family to their home for the next step of their journey, but the pastor replied, "Definitely not! We could lose our lives for that Jewish child!" Corrie's father Casper ten Boom picked up the baby and held it tenderly in his arms: "You say we could lose our lives for this child. I would consider that the greatest honor that could come to my family."

Soon the ten Booms were faced with refugees who were difficult to place in other safe houses, people too old or too sick to travel or with such strongly Semitic features that they could not be disguised safely. They decided they needed to provide some permanent shelter within their own home, so they constructed the "hiding place" up in Corrie's third floor bedroom, the furthest point from the door where searching police might enter. An elderly cantor from a local synagogue, Meyer Mossel, was their first permanent hide-away guest. Mossel and Casper ten Boom would recite the Psalms together. Eventually a core group of seven fugitives joined their family household along with the on-going steady flow of visitors who would stay for just a few nights.

The ten Boom family not only hid the Jews but honored their culture and faith. The entire household kept the Sabbath. They celebrated Hanukkah. They prepared kosher food as long as possible until the time when food shortages left them without meat for weeks. When Corrie's sister Betsie secured some sausage for the hungry household, Mossel said, "There's a provision for this in the Talmud … and I'm going to start hunting for it, too, just as soon as dinner's over!" The graciousness of these Jews and Christians living intimately together under grave threat brought much joy and even humor amid the fear and anxiety.

In February 1944 someone betrayed the family to the German Gestapo. The house was raided, and a trap set to seize anyone who came to the house throughout the day. Thirty people in all were arrested, but the hiding place was not found. The four Jews and two Dutch underground workers who had been hustled into the hiding place stayed in that cramped wall cavity for 47 hours until the underground finally rescued them. Three of the four Jews who had been hiding during the raid and one of the underground members survived the war.

Meanwhile, Corrie ten Boom and her family were taken to a series of prisons and concentration camps. Caspar ten Boom died within ten days. Corrie's nephew Christian ten Boom died in Bergen Belsen. Her brother Willem, an ordained Protestant minister, died shortly after the war from tuberculosis he contracted in prison. Corrie and Betsie were sent to the notorious Ravensbruck concentration camp. As she was dying from starvation and disease Betsie told Corrie, "There is no pit so deep that God's love is not deeper still." On December 30, 1944, Corrie ten Boom was freed from Ravensbruck on what appeared to be an administrative mistake. She spent the rest of the war recovering from the deprivations she had suffered.

Following the war Corrie established rehabilitation centers for disabled people and for survivors of the Nazi concentration camps and prisons. She began to write down her stories, writing a number of books including *The Hiding Place*, which was later made into a movie. Corrie ten Boom is honored as one of the "Righteous Among the Nations" by the Yad Vashem Holocaust Memorial.

It is estimated that Corrie ten Boom and her family helped rescue about 800 Jews during the Holocaust. She died on her 91st birthday. Jewish friends said that only very blessed people are allowed the special privilege of dying on their birthday. She may have been blessed, but she certainly had been a blessing to many.

? Discussion Questions
Chapters 31-36

What qualities of faith do you think would prompt someone to risk their own life to rescue someone of a different faith? How does your faith community support the development and practice of such qualities? Does the faith of the potential victim matter?

What characteristics of faith do you think would block someone from taking action to help a person from a different faith whose life was at risk? Is there any way you see such characteristics played out in your faith community? What is the result of these barriers?

Is it moral to break the law to provide shelter or refuge for someone if it is not a life-and-death issue? What if the person targeted by authorities would merely be deported or lose property? How do you discern the conditions under which someone facing an injustice should be sheltered or assisted?

What makes a hero? Is there anyone you personally know who has seemed heroic to you? What were the qualities you saw in them that made them heroic? What were the risks they took or the consequences they experienced related to their actions?

The frequently quoted saying from the Jewish Torah that whoever saves a person saves the whole world sounds noble. Do you agree? In what way? Is it overstated? Contrast this teaching with the contemporary slogan, "Think globally, act locally." What might this saying and this slogan be saying to us about our responsibility for our actions?

Irene Sendler who helped rescue Jewish children from the Warsaw Ghetto said, "I could have done more. This regret will follow me to my death." Should she have felt such guilt? What do you think made her both act so heroically yet feel so regretful about her own action?

What do you fear the most? Is there anything in your religious beliefs or faith that helps to counter those fears? Are there spiritual steps you can take to enable you to act in the face of what you fear?

Titus Brandsma said in the concentration camp, "We are here in a dark tunnel but we have to go on. At the end, the eternal light is shining for us." What is the role of hope in taking courageous action? Can we act without hope? How does your religious faith speak about hope or strengthen hope?

Imam ben Ghabrit said of the Jews, "Their children are like our own children." How important is personal identification and empathy for mobilizing you to caring action? What things help us feel connected to people in need? What things lessen that connection or make us feel alienated from those in need or danger?

Betsie ten Boom told her sister, "There is no pit so deep that God's love is not deeper still." What in your faith helps you deal with difficulties? Is there an extreme intensity of struggle or trauma that you can imagine would shake that faith? What is the sustaining strength that enables faith to prevail and stirs us to act with compassion and courage in times of extreme duress?

CHAPTER 37

Building Just and Peaceful Communities

Practicing Together What We Preach

Jesus instructed his followers to pray to God, "Thy will be done, thy kingdom come, on earth as it is in heaven." Christians all across the globe pray those words, indicating their desire that the ideal found in heaven be made concrete where we live here on earth. Every religion has a vision of what is good, whether the release from cycles of suffering in Buddhism or the delights of paradise in Islam or the day when "nation shall not lift up sword against nation, neither shall they learn war any more" in the Hebrew prophets Isaiah and Micah. Each religion has its ethical teachings for trying to move humanity toward that ideal in some way, the means for bringing heaven to earth — or the future into the present. Across the street from the United Nations headquarters in New York City the words of the Hebrew prophet Isaiah are chiseled into stone. These words have been the focus of many religious and interfaith

The "Isaiah Wall" in Manhattan, opposite the United Nations Building

vigils for peace, appealing to the leaders of our nations to take steps toward that prophetic vision.

Interreligious conflict and violence can make a hell on earth. Certainly there is a long list of historical examples of religious people acting badly in the name of their God. But religious passions also bring out the best in people. Think about the way people respond to natural disasters. Religious relief agencies, drawing upon resources gathered in local congregations, are usually quicker and freer in providing these resources than governmental agencies. Religious convictions lead many people to extreme levels of dedication, commitment and sacrifice in dealing with some of the daunting problems that face humanity. Religious faith deals with ultimate concerns, so on the basis of those convictions people of faith sometimes take ultimate risks for what is good and right.

During the Crusades, the Christian monk Francis of Assisi and the Muslim sultan al-Malik al-Kamil (both featured in *Interfaith Heroes*) strove to find peace amid the violence of that era. Though they did not bring a halt to the wars, they did create a small vision in their relationship of the peaceful community that could be, across the lines of difference. Their actions still inspire a thousand years later. Individuals have taken prophetic stands against the prevailing norms of the day to call people to a higher standard of behavior as a human family.

In the 20th Century, broad movements for nonviolent change often were founded and shaped by people with religious convictions. Mahatma Gandhi, Abdul Gaffar Khan and Martin Luther King, Jr. showed us both theory and action. Each man was rooted in his own religious faith, yet pursued dynamic dialog with the faiths of others amid political and social struggle. In their footsteps, a host of activists follow, drawing on the nonviolent practices, principles and inspiration from various religious traditions. The newer generations of religious peacemakers include people like Aung San Suu Kyi in Burma (Myanmar), Mubarak Awad from Palestine, Mahmoud Mahomed Taha from Sudan, Desmond Tutu from South

Africa, Adolfo Perez Esquivel from Argentina, Daniel and Philip Berrigan in the United States, Hildegard and Jean Goss-Meyr from Austria and France, Dom Helder Camera from Brazil, Oscar Romero from El Salvador, and so many others whose faith fueled their work for justice and peace.

Some of the struggles for justice and peace were primarily political in nature with religious faith providing the inspiration and determination to shape political actions in nonviolent ways. The International Fellowship of Reconciliation (IFOR) has linked peace fellowships from many different religions to work together, teach each other and support one another in nonviolent struggles for justice and peace. (Muriel Lester, featured in *Interfaith Heroes*, was an International Traveling Secretary for IFOR.)

In 1970 in Kyoto, Japan, the First World Assembly of the World Conference of Religions for Peace was held. The gathering developed when some senior leaders in the major religions began talking about a "religious summit" to explore how religious people around the world could take action for peace. A series of assemblies was held with the Eighth World Assembly returning to in Kyoto in 2006. That year, 2,000 participants gathered from over 100 countries. Together they rejected the "hijacking" of religions as an excuse for violence. As Religions for Peace, they developed an on-going structure and program to facilitate interreligious projects in troubled areas, seeking to transform conflicts, address poverty and mobilize women and youth for peace.

First World Assembly of the World Conference of Religions, Kyoto, 1970

The 21st Century has dawned with religion as a major factor in global life. The fate of our planet depends to a large extent on how religious leaders — from grassroots communities to global denominations — decide to engage with other faiths. Will these leaders choose conflict and even violence? Or will they risk crossing boundaries to work toward peace? The interfaith heroes in this section can guide us.

CHAPTER 38

Charles Freer Andrews
(1871-1940)

C hrist's Faithful Apostle. That was the name given to this Christian priest by the Hindu Indian independence leader Mahatma Gandhi, playing off the initials of Charles Freer Andrews. Andrews was one of Gandhi's closest associates and friends. Together they struggled for justice and freedom over many years and in many settings.

Andrews grew up in England, studied at Cambridge, became an Anglican priest and then was named Vice Principal of Westcott House Theological College at Cambridge. Since his college days he had been involved in struggles for justice as part of his understanding of the Christian gospel. He looked especially at issues related to his own country and injustices in the British Empire, particularly in India.

He moved to India, joined the Cambridge Brotherhood in Delhi and became a professor of philosophy at St. Stephen's College. He witnessed first-hand the racist treatment of Indians by the British and began to write in support of Indian aspirations for independence. He joined the Indian National Congress and helped resolve the cotton workers' strike in Madras in 1913.

One of the Indian political leaders asked Andrews to go to South Africa to assist in the political struggles of the Indian community in that country. There he met Mohandas Gandhi, a young lawyer seeking to organize Indians to deal by nonviolent means with the discrimination they faced in South Africa. Andrews saw the Christian values he held dear reflected in Gandhi's teaching of *ahimsa* or "total nonviolence." Andrews helped Gandhi organize his Ashram and publish the journal *The Indian Opinion*.

In 1916, Gandhi and Andrews returned together to India to work for Indian independence. Andrews worked with the trade unions and joined in the Vaikkom Temple protests in support of the so-called "untouchables." As part of the independence struggle, he particularly focused on a series of dialogues between Christians and Hindus. Andrews accompanied Gandhi back to London for the Round Table Conference in 1930 to assist Gandhi in negotiations with the British.

Throughout this period, Christian missionaries had called attention to the plight of the Indian indentured laborers in Fiji. Andrews went to Fiji with W.W. Pearson, and their report led to halting further transportation of Indian labor to British colonies. Though this was an improvement, the condition of those workers in Fiji and other colonies was still abysmal. Andrews' further trip to Fiji and subsequent protests helped lead to the abolishment of the entire system of Indian indentured labor in 1920.

As the movement for Indian independence gathered strength, Gandhi felt it was time for sympathetic British friends such as Andrews to step aside. The leadership of the movement needed to be fully Indian. So, steeped in the teachings and action of Gandhi, Andrews departed from India and spent more time in Britain. He focused on teaching the next generation about living out Christ's call to radical discipleship through nonviolent struggles for justice and freedom.

Chapter 39

Dorothy Day
(1897-1980)

Don't call me a saint. I don't want to be dismissed so easily.

Dorothy Day was once a Communist who became a leading voice for radical nonviolent Christianity in the United States. She lived a life of voluntary poverty, cared for the homeless, published *The Catholic Worker* newspaper and founded a movement by the same name that continues to this day.

Day's early adulthood was spent as a muckraking leftist journalist, joining herself with various protest movements and embracing the sexual revolution of the 1920s. Faced with her second pregnancy, she was spurred onto a religious quest that ended with her conversion to Catholicism, abandoning her lover and keeping her baby. She also kept her passion for the poor and struggles for justice that had marked her earlier years, but now that passion was wedded to a deep spirituality.

In 1933, she met Peter Maurin and they co-founded *The Catholic Worker* to address concerns of war and poverty from a radical Catholic perspective. The press run for their first issue was only 2,500 copies, but by the end of the year they were publishing 100,000 copies per issue. They sold their paper for a penny so that anyone could afford it, but even so they still gave away thousands of copies. The paper didn't just criticize what was going on in the world; it challenged readers to make a personal response. Most of the writing initially came directly from Dorothy Day herself.

She and Maurin founded the House of Hospitality to feed the hungry and shelter the homeless in New York City. That house was the first in what grew to be many Catholic Worker Houses across the country. Before Mother Teresa picked up the dying in Calcutta, Dorothy Day was welcoming the poorest of the poor, the destitute, addicted and dying into the Catholic Worker Houses. She said, "Once they are taken in, they become members of the family. Or rather they always were members of the family. They are our brothers and sisters in Christ." Religion or background did not matter, only that a person was in need.

In 1936, the Spanish Civil War erupted. Her old leftist friends supported the Republican side while most American Catholics supported Franco and the Fascists. Day took a different approach — nonviolence, rooted in the gospels. When she later learned of Gandhi, who had influenced some of her colleagues, she began to incorporate his ideas into her writings. Instead of the "holy war" of the Catholics or the "holy revolution" of the Communists, she lifted up Gandhi's nonviolent methodology for struggling for justice and against the wars waged by both nations and revolutionary causes. During the Cold War anxieties of the 1950s and 1960s she was jailed three times for refusing to participate in civil defense drills in New York. She protested the draft and the war in Vietnam. She was last jailed at the age of 75 for taking part in a banned picket in support of striking farm workers. Day also was nearly hit by rifle fire from the Klu Klux Klan while supporting the racially integrated community of Koinonia Farms in Georgia in 1957 when bullets smashed into the steering column of the car she was driving.

Dorothy Day was a strong voice against anti-Semitism as Hitler was rising to power in Europe. *The Catholic Worker* was certainly the first Catholic journal, maybe one of the first non-Jewish papers in the U.S., to decry the persecution of the

Jews growing under the Nazis. She was one of the founders of Catholics to Fight Anti-Semitism. She became a staunch critic of Father Charles Coughlin, the fiery priest who used his radio programs to promote anti-Semitic ideas and who promoted the spurious "Protocols of the Elders of Zion" in his journal *Social Justice*. Day could be pointedly acerbic in her critiques of such hate speech, especially from a religious source.

As her health failed, she was given many honors. Mother Teresa was one of the people who came to visit her. But Dorothy Day brushed off such attention: "Don't call me a saint. I don't want to be dismissed so easily." Theodore Hesburgh of Notre Dame University said Day was known for "comforting the afflicted and afflicting the comfortable" as he presented her the Laetare Medal for her social witness.

Chapter 40

Stephen Samuel Wise
(1874-1949)

> *What is happening in Germany today may happen tomorrow in any other land on earth unless it is challenged and rebuked.*

Stephen Wise was a rabbi rooted deeply in Jewish faith and politics. He was passionate about Jewish affairs and survival, but his passions also broadened to working class people and the poor and victims of discrimination of any race, class or religion.

Wise came from a family of rabbis. Born in Budapest, at that time part of the Austro-Hungarian Empire, his family moved to New York when he was an infant. The family name Weiss was Anglicized to Wise. He studied for the rabbinate serving as rabbi in Oregon and New York. He was invited to be the rabbi at the prestigious Temple Emanu-El but turned the offer down when the congregation would not give him a "free pulpit" where he could speak as he was led by his conscience and understanding of the Jewish faith. So, in 1907 he founded the Free Synagogue in New York City where there were no restrictions of any kind placed on the pulpit. He stayed at the Free Synagogue for 43 years.

Wise plunged into many social causes. He supported ordinary workers in their labor struggles, such as the Brooklyn transit strike. The terrible fire at the Triangle Shirt Factory in 1911 that killed 146 women deeply shook Rabbi Wise, and he joined in the fight against sweatshops and for safe working conditions. He participated in many labor-management disputes, offering his services as a mediator.

These struggles for social justice brought Rabbi Wise into partnership with people of other religions, especially Christians acting for reform out of the "social gospel" movement. He engaged in many interfaith activities as well as activities in the public sector that involved alliances with people of different social groups. Out of his concern for justice, in 1906 Wise was one of the founders of the National Association for the Advancement of Colored Peoples (NAACP) that became one of the most storied U.S. civil rights organizations. He was a key organizer of the American Jewish Congress in 1918 that mobilized Jewish leaders to work for equal rights of all Americans regardless of race, religion or national origin.

Wise was a leader within Reformed Judaism, educating rabbis through the founding of the Jewish Institute of Religion, which later became Hebrew Union College. He was an early leader in the Zionist movement, participating in the formation of the Federation of American Zionists. As Adolph Hitler came to power in Germany, Wise became concerned with the persecution of the Jews. He worked to mobilize public opinion in the U.S. against the Nazis and became an advisor to President Franklin D. Roosevelt about Jewish issues. Rabbi Wise and Leo Motzkin led in founding the World Jewish Congress to take on the issues of rising Nazism and sought a boycott of Nazi Germany. Wise insisted that Jews become their own advocates and not just criticize the Christians for allowing the rise of Hitler: "How can we ask our Christian friends to lift their voices in protest against the wrongs suffered by Jews if we keep silent? What is happening in Germany today may happen tomorrow in any other land on earth unless it is challenged and rebuked."

Chapter 41

Masahisa Goi
(1916-1980)

"**M**ay peace prevail on earth." That simple prayer has been "planted" in many languages on more than 200,000 "Peace Poles" around the world. It is a prayer that bridges religious and linguistic divisions, bringing people together in a common expression of prayer and hope for peace.

The visionary behind the World Peace Prayer was the Japanese philosopher and spiritual leader Masahisa Goi. As a child Goi was very frail, so to deal with his poor health he began to explore the disciplines of yoga, spiritual healing and the martial arts. He engaged in long periods of meditation. During World War II he worked in a factory, but outside of his work he organized various cultural events including a choir. The war was a traumatic spiritual experience for him, and he began to yearn desperately for peace, not only for Japan but for the world.

Goi founded Byakko Shinko Kai, an organization to promote spiritual practices dedicated to world peace. He studied teachings of various religions including the Chinese philosopher Lao Tsu and the Bible. Through his books and lectures he encouraged people to seek inner peace as well as world peace.

In a long journey of prayer in which he asked to be of service to humanity, he believed the prayer "May peace prevail on earth" was given to him. He believed if people put their efforts into this prayer for peace it would help to unite humanity. In 1955, he founded the Movement of Prayer for World Peace, which eventually became the World Peace Prayer Society. It was intentionally established as a movement to transcend all religious, social, ethnic and political barriers through the promotion of the prayer. "Peace Poles" were designed to be inscribed with the prayer in various languages. These poles would then be set into the ground as constant reminders and witnesses to the hope for peace. Peace Poles have been planted in every country, in ordinary places such as houses of worship and homes and in places of special conflict. Many religious leaders have planted Peace Poles including Pope John Paul II, Mother Teresa and the Dalai Lama. Masahisa Goi's simple prayer has become an inspiration to millions of people around the world who have never heard his name but have shared his passion and hope.

To obtain information about Peace Poles in the United States, contact Peace Pole Makers USA at www.PeacePoles.com or at 7221 S. Wheeler Rd., Maple City, Michigan 49664 (phone: 231-334-4567). For other sources around the world contact: http://www.worldpeace.org/peacepoles.html.

Chapter 42

Richard St. Barbe Baker
(1889-1982)

I am determined to live and work for peaceful construction for I am morally responsible for the world of today and the generations of tomorrow.

"The Man of the Trees" he was called, first by the Kikuyu people in Kenya. He had gone to Kenya to study the effects of centuries of land mismanagement. He set up a tree nursery, utilizing native species. His work of healing the land in partnership with the Kikuyus led to his becoming the first white person inducted into the secret society of Kikuyu Elders. He was given the name *Watu wa Miti*, "The Man of the Trees," an appellation that became the name of an international organization.

Richard St. Barbe Barker grew up in England, loving the outdoors whether he worked in the garden or roamed through the forest. While doing missionary work in western Canada he became convinced that agricultural practices were degrading the soil and destroying the prairie. So he returned to England to study forestry at Cambridge. After suspending his studies to serve in World War I, he graduated and went to Kenya to begin his first reforestation project in 1922.

In 1924 he returned to England and was introduced to the Bahá'í Faith. He studied the religion and embraced it. Throughout his life St. Barbe was a dedicated practitioner of the Bahá'í faith, but he also had a deep affinity and respect for the animism of many of the indigenous people around the world with whom he worked closely. He wrote, "It is with a spirit of reverence that I approach God's creation, this beautiful Earth." He mourned the desacralization of Creation, turning Nature into a commodity for exploitation.

St. Barbe began to travel around the world developing his Men of the Trees organization. Eventually there were chapters in more than 100 countries, pursuing projects of reforestation and land restoration. In the United States he worked with President Franklin Roosevelt to establish the Civilian Conservation Corps that eventually mobilized 6 million youths in conservation projects. He envisioned a massive project to reclaim the Sahara Desert through strategic planting of trees, making a groundbreaking ecological survey in his 60s. Even at the age of 91, St. Barbe traveled to the Himalayas to join in the Chipko movement of peasant women in India seeking to protect trees.

Following his participation in the First World Forestry Congress in Rome in 1926, St. Barbe went to Palestine to set up a chapter of Men of the Trees. He gained the support of Shoghi Effendi, the Guardian of the Bahá'í Faith, who became the first life member of Men of the Trees in Palestine. St. Barbe then organized an interfaith coalition of Muslims, Jews and Christians as well as Bahá'ís to organize reforestation projects in Palestine.

As St. Barbe worked with religious people around the world, the task of healing the land was a task of spiritual renewal. He spoke of Nature as "holy," as a "sentient being." He wrote, "I am determined to live and work for peaceful construction for I am morally responsible for the world of today and the generations of tomorrow."

Chapter 43

Thich Nhat Hanh
(b. 1926)

Nhat Hanh was born in central Vietnam. At the age of 16 he became a novice studying Buddhism, then was ordained as a monk in 1949. *Thich* was added to his name, which identifies Vietnamese Buddhist monks and nuns who are part of the Shakyamuni Buddhist clan.

Thich Nhat Hanh became the editor of *Vietnamese Buddhism* and founded Van Hanh Buddhist University, which specialized in Buddhist studies and Vietnamese language and cultural studies. He went to Princeton to further his studies in comparative religion. However, the growing war in Vietnam drew him back to his homeland to join with other Buddhist monks in nonviolent peace initiatives.

In the 1960s, Thich Nhat Hanh founded the School of Youth for Social Services (SYSS). This was a grassroots relief organization that mobilized 10,000 Vietnamese young people to rebuild villages that had been bombed, resettle displaced families and set up schools and medical clinics.

In 1966 he returned to the U.S., specifically to work for peace. He met Martin Luther King, Jr., with whom he had carried on an earlier correspondence. He urged King to publicly denounce the war in Vietnam. In 1967 Dr. King gave his famous speech at Riverside Church in New York City where he condemned the war and the "giant triplets of racism, materialism and militarism." In the speech he referred to the peace witness of the Vietnamese Buddhists. King, as a Nobel Laureate, nominated Thich Nhat Hanh for the Nobel Peace Prize that year saying, "I do not personally know of anyone more worthy of [this prize] than this gentle monk from Vietnam. His ideas for peace, if applied, would build a monument to ecumenism, to world brotherhood, to humanity." Though Thich Nhat Hanh was not awarded the prize, he continued his work for peace, serving as a delegate for the Buddhist Peace Delegation at the Paris Peace talks.

As the war was winding down Thich Nhat Hanh was not allowed to return to Vietnam. In exile he worked to help rescue the boat people fleeing his homeland. He settled in France, establishing a meditation center that eventually was known as Plum Village Buddhist Center. There he taught classes on a wide range of topics, led retreats, and applied "mindfulness" to the various problems of the world. He welcomed people from all religions, nationalities and races to the center.

He was one of the founders and leaders of the International Network of Engaged Buddhists that seeks to engage in the inner transformation that brings healing to the world. Through this network he and other Buddhists joined with religious peace fellowships through the International Fellowship of Reconciliation where Thich Nhat Hanh has often been a featured speaker and writer. Among his 85 books of poetry, prayers, meditations and prose is *Living Buddha Living Christ* in which Thich Nhat Hanh explored ways of reconciling Christianity and Buddhism. He has been welcomed into Christian and Jewish settings to speak on issues of peace, forgiveness and active nonviolence. He sponsored a retreat for Israelis and Palestinians to listen and learn about each other.

In 2005 and again in 2007 he was finally allowed to return for a visit to his homeland after more than 30 years of exile. He continues as a voice for peace and for a healing mindfulness about the challenges of the world.

CHAPTER 44

Karim Al-Hussayni, Aga Khan IV
(b. 1936)

This Muslim Prince of Pakistani origin has lived most of his life traveling around the world. As a person with global exposure since childhood he has become a leader in a worldwide educational movement to equip people to live in a diverse world rather than give in to the fears of a "clash of civilizations."

Karim al-Hussayni was born into the family of a royal Pakistani independence leader who was living in Geneva, Switzerland, at the time of his birth. His childhood was spent in Kenya, creating a lasting love and concern for Africa. Then he returned to Switzerland and later went to Harvard University in the U.S. to complete his schooling, already spanning three continents.

His grandfather was Aga Khan III, the Imam of the Shia Ismaili Muslims, a religious community of about 20 million people. The elder Imam named his grandson as his successor, now to be designated as Aga Khan IV, because of the fundamental changes taking place in a rapidly globalizing world. He saw Karim al-Hussayni as someone uniquely able to bring experience and new perspective to his religious leadership. So at the age of 20 Aga Khan IV assumed leadership of the Ismaili Muslims.

In addition to his role as a religious leader, Aga Khan IV is a billionaire who has turned his assests into a campaign to eliminate global poverty especially through education. He established the Aga Khan Development Network with nine inter-related agencies to pursue various development projects in poorer countries as well as emergency relief activities. For Aga Khan, the challenge is to make development sustainable and equitable, benefiting all classes, cultures and regions of the world fairly. In various educational programs and the Aga Khan Academies across South Asia, Africa and the Middle East, students are supported regardless of race, gender or religious background. In Afghanistan his projects have been especially noted for educating Afghani girls.

Aga Khan's premier educational initiative has been the International Baccalaureate Organization (IB) established to improve education in poor countries particularly in an effort to help young people adapt to a diverse multi-cultural world. The IB mission statement says, "The International Baccalaureate aims to develop inquiring, knowledgeable and caring young people who help to create a better and more peaceful world through intercultural understanding and respect. ... These programs encourage students across the world to become active, compassionate and lifelong learners who understand that other people, with their differences, can also be right." IB programs have helped more than 650,000 students in 2,400 schools in 129 countries over the 40 years of the program to date.

For Aga Khan, the tolerance that embraces diversity is rooted in his religious faith. He speaks of the Quranic view of all humanity as sharing an origin as children of God. Building positive relationships with people who are different and cooperating with people of other faiths and races will help build harmony in the world. Not content to rest upon what he has accomplished, Aga Khan continues to dream of new ways to encourage the diverse peoples of the world to learn about one another and live together peacefully. He is planning a Global Center for Pluralism to be opened in Canada that will promote Islamic awareness and a pluralistic attitude in society.

CHAPTER 45

Sulak Sivaraksa
(b. 1933)

Those who want to change society must understand the inner dimensions of change. It is this sense of personal transformation that religion can provide.

Questioning. That word helps to define the life of Sulak Sivaraksa. He views his religion of Buddhism as a questioning process. Question everything, he says, including oneself. We must look deeply into ourselves, then act from that insight. For Sulak, deep spirituality can ignite social engagement for transformative change.

Born in 1933 in Thailand, Sulak began his social work by editing *Social Science Review* magazine and seeking sustainable development models for rapid social and economic change. His work with Buddhist monks and student activists led to the founding of many organizations including the Coordinating Group for Religion and Society and the Thai Inter-Religious Commission for Development (TICD). He co-founded the International Network of Engaged Buddhists with other Buddhist activists such as the Dalai Lama and Thich Nhat Hanh.

In 1976, a bloody military coup in which hundreds of students were killed forced Sulak into exile for two years. After returning to Thailand he was arrested in 1984 for criticizing the king, but international protests prompted the government to release him. When, in 1991, he challenged the repression of democracy in Thailand he was once again forced into exile until the courts, in 1995, established his innocence of any crime.

Sulak's Thai Inter-Religious Commission for Development has involved Buddhist monks and nuns in issues of ethics, community development, ecology and various social, political and economic issues. Based upon Buddhist principles of community building and social change, TICD has promoted religious dialogues among Buddhists, Muslims and Christians in Thailand on topics including peace and nonviolence. In the southern provinces of Thailand where Buddhist-Muslim violence has been severe, TICD has promoted dialogue as well as advocated for Muslim and Christian concerns. In 2007, Sulak spoke against proposed constitutional changes that would make Buddhism the national religion of Thailand, knowing such a move would deepen the conflicts with the Muslim community. TICD also expanded the interreligious dialogues with neighbors in Malaysia and Indonesia.

In 1995, Sulak founded the Spirit in Education Movement (SEM), an alternative university for developing grassroots leaders in marginalized communities. SEM's philosophy is based on Buddhist wisdom and views on ecological sustainability, social justice and nonviolence. Sulak brought Quakers, Catholics and Hindus onto the faculty to foster creative interaction through their various spiritually based viewpoints on global change.

For Sulak, there is no split between the inner life of contemplation and the outer life of social activism. Both are essential as the inner and the outer aspects of religious life illuminate, inform and encourage each other. In fact, the inner spirituality is essential for true transformation to take place in society. He wrote "that radical transformation of society requires personal and spiritual change first or at least simultaneously has been accepted by Buddhists and many other religious adherents for more than 2,500 years. Those who want to change society must understand the inner dimensions of change. It is this sense of personal transformation that religion can provide. ... There are many descriptions of the religious experience, but all come back to becoming less and less selfish."

CHAPTER 46

Patricia Smith Melton
(b. 1942)

Hope is based as much in stubbornness as it is in dreams. Don't let anyone take it away from you.

In January 2002, six women gathered for a three-day forum on the topic: "What is peace, and how can women be empowered to bring it in?" The women were from different religious beliefs, cultures and life experiences, but they all were viewed as leading figures in the areas of peace and women's rights. Their gathering was conceived in a hotel room in San Francisco on September 18, 2001, days after the terrorist attacks of September 11th. Patricia Smith Melton was awakened from her sleep with a deep sense of a palpable presence. She felt she had been given an assignment by the presence to work through women to bring peace. A few months later the first women's circle had gathered.

That circle launched a movement that became Peace X Peace (read aloud as "peace by peace"). At the heart of Peace X Peace are circles of women that connect to other circles through the Internet. They share about their cultures and their actions for peace, providing each other mutual support and encouragement. In just a few short years,

Peace X Peace has grown exponentially with circles in more than 100 countries. The vision of this growing women's movement is that by joining together they can develop the critical mass of consciousness to shift societies around the world from violence and war toward the peaceful resolution of conflicts.

Patricia Smith Melton had a full career as an artist, writing plays and poetry and working as a photographer. She continues to use art, including documentary filming, as part of her peace work. Her documentary "Peace X Peace: Women on the Frontlines" premiered at the United Nations, received two film awards and was broadcast on more than 300 public television stations.

In 1991 Smith Melton and her husband William Melton established the Melton Foundation. The mission of the foundation is "to build a world-wide community of talented people from diverse cultures capable of addressing global issues based on principles of open communication and mutual respect." To carry out this mission the foundation sponsors various activities for people to gather together both face-to-face and in on-line cyber-communities for cross-cultural training and social-professional interaction. For Smith Melton, the values of relationship and communication are central to bringing about positive change in the world, and these values have shaped both the work of the Melton Foundation and the vision of Peace X Peace. The divides of religion, culture and inequality can be bridged as people encounter one another and learn from each other.

This work of connecting people for the long-term goal of peace is a spiritual calling, she says. Smith Melton was raised in a mainstream Protestant church. She speaks of a creative "triangle" in her life of "spiritual awareness, pain in the world, and inner freedom." That triangle of spirituality, pain and freedom is part of what inspires her to connect women of different religious faiths, nationalities and backgrounds so that they can collaborate for peaceful positive change in the world. But her dreams are not all the sweet fluff of peace. She says, "Hope is based as much in stubbornness as it is in dreams. Don't let anyone take it away from you."

In her latest project, Smith Melton has sought to address what she calls "the world's deepest wound," the division between Christians, Jews and Muslims in Israel and Palestine. She has worked on bridging cultural-religious divides in the Middle East with a particular focus on the role of women in transforming the conflicts. A book, *Sixty Years, Sixty Voices*, collecting the voices of sixty Israeli and Palestinian women, is the fruit of her efforts to connect to women and open the channels of communication.

Patricia Smith Melton envisions a transformation in the world in which a more powerful voice is heard from those most marginalized—women. For her, ordinary people are extraordinary, so the telling of their stories unleashes powerful forces for change. Using today's technology through film and the Internet, these voices and stories can support transformative action around the world.

Chapter 47

Gaston Grandjean Dayanand

Gaston Grandjean is one of the most humble heroes imaginable. His work is so inspiring that the main character in Dominique Lapierre's novel *City of Joy* was based on him, even though Grandjean did not want himself to be visible. However, the success of *City of Joy* and the subsequent movie by that name have brought his work amid the anonymity of Calcutta's slums to worldwide awareness.

Grandjean was born in Switzerland. He grew up wanting to be a missionary, but he was discouraged on the grounds that his health was too fragile. However, he had little concern for his own health and, when his first vocation seemed to be blocked, he went to work in the coal mines of northern France with immigrants from Turkey, Algeria and Yugoslavia. Then he worked in the steel mills of Paris. These exposures to the working poor developed a life-long passion to serve the poor.

Grandjean finally trained as a nurse and then joined the Prado Fraternity. Prado is a Catholic order that brings together both "religious" (monks and nuns) and consecrated lay people who are willing to take a vow to "join the poorest of the poor and the most disinherited where they are, live the same life as they do and die with them." He worked in Latin America, Africa and Asia, but it was India where he found his true calling. He settled in Howrah, one of the worst slums of Calcutta, making his simple home among the people he sought to serve. His only belongings were a Bible, a razor and a toothbrush.

Known as Brother Gaston, he helped the residents of Howrah with their various needs, including health. He overcame their distrust because he didn't seek to proselytize. Rather he entered into the lives and rituals of all those in the slum, whether they were Muslim, Hindu or Christian. He formed the Southern Health Improvement Samity (SHIS) in 1980 through which he trained social workers and health workers from the slums. Eventually he founded an Interreligious Centre as a place for the marginalized in special distress to receive care and to be a place to apprentice social workers from all religious backgrounds. For example, Dr. Mohammed Kamrudin, a young Muslim who started a center for humanitarian action in Calcutta, was inspired, mentored and trained by Brother Gaston.

Brother Gaston also established Shanti Bhavan, the Inter-Religious Centre of Development. Shanti Bhavan is a home for the destitute, for orphans and for the menally challenged. Now an older man, the people of the home call him Dadu, grandfather, as he cares for them dressed in his simple kurta-pyjama pants.

Brother Gaston took the Indian name of Dayanand. In 1992, Gaston Dayanand became a citizen of India, fully rooted in the poor communities of Calcutta, known now worldwide by the name "City of Joy."

CHAPTER 48

Ahangamage Tudor Ariyaratne
(b. 1931)

We build the road, and the road builds us.

Ahangamage Tudor Ariyaratne, better known as A.T. Ariyaratne, stands the trickle-down approach on its head. He advocates for and practices "development from the bottom up." Ariyaratne has an academic background, but he has put his beliefs into practice to such an extent that he has created the largest non-governmental organization in Sri Lanka, a movement that has garnered worldwide attention and acclaim.

Ariyarante is a deeply devout Buddhist who has fused the teachings of the Buddha with the activist philosophy of Gandhi to develop a potent and broad approach to the complex problems experienced by the poor of his country. He built a foundation for his work from the "five precepts": Non-killing, non-stealing, non-sexual indulgence, nonviolence and non-intoxication. Then he sought to inculcate the expressions of character in Buddha's four characteristics: "To practice loving kindness toward all living beings, to engage yourself in compassionate action, to gain joy out of serving other people and to work in a spirit of equality." Out of these Buddhist principles he set forth principles for their work in the community: sharing, pleasant language of compassion and respect, constructive activity, and equality of association.

In the late 1950s, this college professor decided that students needed to move out of the classroom into the villages of Sri Lanka. He challenged students to give 10 days of labor a year to the poorest villages as an extension of their education. The experience was transformative for the students and the villagers as pressing needs were met by people working together. The project grew to 100 villages in 1967, and kept growing to 15,000 villages by 2001.

The organization formed by Ariyarante to facilitate this work is Sarvodaya Shramadana, which means "the sharing of labor, thought and energy for the awakening of all." The grassroots movement of Sarvodaya begins with community organizing, helping people to learn to work collaboratively to identify their needs and decide what is most important to address first. People in a village work together on the Gandhian principle of direct self-governance. Then people are mobilized from across Sri Lanka and even from around the world to labor on these projects. Together people have built thousands of schools, community health centers, libraries, cottage industries, wells and latrines. Three hundred small village banks have been established that together have as much in assets as any large commercial bank in Sri Lanka. Irrigation projects, solar energy projects and programs that promote biodiversity have been established. People come together to work from all religions, castes, ages and economic levels, and together they are transformed. As the Sarvodaya motto puts it: "We build the road, and the road builds us."

All this has been done through mobilizing ordinary people through their renewed spirituality. Ariyaratne speaks out of his own Buddhist tradition and has brought many local Buddhist monks into an active role in transforming village life. But he also has engaged Hindus, Christians and Muslims to work alongside Buddhists as part of living out the principle of equality of association. He calls people to "try to awaken themselves spiritually and thus transcend sectarian religious difference, to become one with all."

In a country that has been torn by a long, bloody civil war along ethnic and religious lines, Ariyaratne has been a tireless peacemaker. He took the Sarvodaya movement to the Jaffna Penisula, the Tamil-dominated area at the heart of the conflict. As a part of their development work, the members of Sarvodaya teach and model the principles of nonviolence, especially through the interpretations of Gandhi. Ariyaratne's blend of the teachings of Buddha and Gandhi is a powerful antidote to the conflict that has pitted a Tamil Hindu minority against the Sinhalese Buddhist majority.

Ariyaratne has also launched massive peace walks in which he asks people to come together to meditate on peace. Buddhist monks, Hindu swamis, Catholic nuns and lay people from all faiths have gathered in various locations around Sri Lanka to meditate. The movement has grown from a few thousand to more than 900,000 people meditating on peace together, crossing all the lines of division.

Through the spiritually rooted work of Dr. Ariyaratne and Sarvodaya millions of people in thousands of villages have been transformed, uniting people with a common purpose from various religions, castes and ethnicities. As Ariyaratne likes to say, "We ordinary human beings can make a much greater difference than governments."

CHAPTER 49

Muhammed Nurayn Ashafa and James Movel Wuye

(B. 1960)   (B. 1960)

You cannot cross the ocean with hate in your heart.

The city of Kaduna has been the epicenter of violence between Muslim and Christian communities in northern Nigeria. In 1992, religious riots erupted in which hundreds of people were killed and houses of worship on both sides were destroyed. Muhammed Nurayn Ashafa and James Movel Wuye were on opposite sides of the fighting, playing leading roles stirring up the violence.

Both men were born in 1960 and took parallel paths to leadership among the youth in their respective communities. James Wuye became a mapmaker by profession and a lay evangelist by conviction. He was vice-president of the Youth Christian Association of Nigeria and regularly wrote articles in their newspaper *The Whole Truth*. Muhammed Ashafa became a Muslim preacher and was the Secretary-General of the Kaduna chapter of the National Council of Muslim Youth Organizations.

He also wrote extensively in their news bulletin. Both leaders expressed radical, provocative ideas with uncompromising attitudes. Wuye wanted to totally evangelize Nigeria, and Ashafa worked for the total Islamization of Nigeria. When the violence exploded they were in the forefront of the fighting. Wuye lost an arm from wounds he received. Ashafa's mentor and his brother were both killed. Ashafa's mentor had been a Sufi hermit who once challenged him, "You cannot cross the ocean with hate in your heart." When Christian militiamen murdered the Sufi mystic, Ashafa sought revenge.

In 1995 Wuye and Ashafa encountered each other at a meeting sponsored by a women's organization. As they talked they discovered in spite of their suspicions that they had more in common than they ever imagined. Their images of their "enemy" were shattered, and that day they began a quest to work together to solve the problems of religious conflict in their community. It wasn't easy for them.

During a Friday service at his mosque, Ashafa heard an imam talk about the story of Prophet Muhammad going to preach in Ta'if. Muhammad was rejected, stoned, and left bleeding. When an angel appeared and asked if Muhammad would like to destroy those who had rejected him, Muhammad replied, "No." This story began to work in a healing way in Ashafa's heart, and he wept during the service. To express his forgiveness to Wuye, he visited the ailing aunt of the Christian leader as she was in the hospital.

Meanwhile Wuye struggled with his own bitterness having been left for dead by Muslim attackers who had hacked off his arm. Then, at a conference, ironically featuring a noted anti-Muslim speaker, a pastor challenged Wuye directly with words that echoed the Sufi mystic's message to Ashafa: "You can't preach Jesus with hate in your heart." Wuye says those words "deprogrammed" him.

As former hard-liners it was a difficult task to bring the leadership of their respective organizations into a process of mutual discovery and dialogue, but they began the process.

Visits were made to the meetings of each organization. Wuye visited a mosque, and Ashafa visited a church. Symposia with Christian-Muslim dialogue were held and met with great success.

Eventually, they formed an organization for which they are co-coordinators, the Muslim/Christian Youth Dialogue Forum in Nigeria. This organization has held educational events and published books and pamphlets on interfaith mediation and peace-building. They co-authored *The Pastor and the Imam: Responding to Conflict* that tells their stories, explores the similarities and differences of Christianity and Islam, and calls for Christians and Muslims to work together for understanding and peace. "We planted the seed of genocide, and we used the scripture to do that," Ashafa said, referring to their earlier involvement in the interreligious violence. So, as part of their writing and teaching on reconciliation, they have highlighted the use of their respective scriptures. They use quotes from the Bible and the Quran to explore areas of common belief and areas of disagreement between Christians and Muslims. Then, again quoting extensively from the Quran and the Bible, they show why Muslims and Christians should engage with each other peacefully rather than violently. As they write in the introduction, "Our appeal is that the two religions acknowledge the existence of other faiths and that the adherents of Islam and Christianity live harmoniously with people of other faiths."

These two leaders renamed their organization the Interfaith Mediation Centre. They have conducted many educational events related to peace building and reconciliation across religious lines. They also are active in the streets seeking to quell violence. Once, Imam Ashafa provided shelter in his own home for a Christian woman fleeing violent Muslim youths. Pastor Wuye also saved a Muslim woman at risk from Christian youths who threatened her.

Ashafa and Wuye have become key figures both in Nigeria and around the world in efforts to promote peace between Muslim and Christian communities. They both find some of their harshest critics within their own faiths as disagreements about how to interact with the other faith are very deep and intense. Both Ashafa and Wuye are committed to extending their faiths, even in the other communities. But they acknowledge that they have to find the space for coexistence, a commitment that they discovered was deeply rooted in their own religious traditions.

❓ Discussion Questions
Chapters 37-49

The Hebrew prophet Isaiah presented a vision of people living together in peace, reshaping weapons into agricultural tools, and leaving aside the lessons of war they had been taught for generations. What are the principles, images and visions of the future that help inspire faith-filled actions for people in your religious tradition? What are the principles, images and visions that inspire you personally?

Have you ever worked alongside a person of another faith in a community project of some kind? Was religion directly a part of that project? Did you share with anyone of another faith your religious motivations related to the work — and hear their religious motivations as well? If so, what did you learn?

How does religion get "hijacked" or manipulated for purposes that are antithetical to core religious values? Where have you seen such processes in action? Can you identify examples in which your own faith tradition has been used for some more narrow political purpose? What are appropriate religious motivations for action in the social and political problems that face our global community?

Dorothy Day said, "Don't call me a saint. I don't want to be dismissed so easily." How do we use terms like "heroes" or "saints" to avoid our own responsibilities for right action in the world? What should those terms mean? What enables "heroes" or "saints" to inspire and guide us?

Aga Khan IV and Sulak Sivaraksa made education key components of their efforts to bring positive change to the world. Do you know of exciting educational programs in your local schools or universities that are stimulating creative involvement in social change? A.T. Ariyaratne took students out of the classroom into the villages of Sri Lanka to connect the classroom to the ordinary life of Sri Lankans. What can you do to help people in schools connect theory to practice and the classroom to the neighborhood, the street and the ecosystem?

Muhammed Ashafa and James Wuye formed a partnership as a Muslim and a Christian leader to deal with a major point of social division. Where might such partnerships be formed to help with issues in your community? What steps could you take to initiate such a partnership? What risks might you incur in crossing lines of division?

Each hero in this section was drawn to a particular issue or vision. What are the passions that stir your heart? What issues burn most brightly inside you? How do you nurture that inner fire? What steps have you taken to follow through on what is in your heart? Who might be your allies or partners in the work you feel moved to do?

Sulak Sivaraksa speaks of the transformation of both the inner and the outer aspects of the spiritual life. The radical transformation of society cannot take place unless there is first or at least simultaneously transformation of the inner person. How do you connect your inner journey of spirituality with efforts to bring about constructive change in the world? How does what you do flow out of the center of who you are? What spiritual practices nourish that potent personal center in you?

Chapter 50

It's Our Turn Now
Interfaith Partners Stories And Challenges

The nightmare began when two planes flew into skyscrapers. The dream began on a yacht on the Detroit River. Sparked by the nightmare and the dream, Interfaith Partners was born: a network of religious people of different faiths in metropolitan Detroit seeking to build a more healthy community together, beginning in southeast Michigan but touching distant places in the world.

The night after the September 11, 2001, terrorist attacks, a large number of Christian, Muslim and Jewish leaders, mostly clergy along with a few lay leaders, gathered at a mosque in Dearborn, Michigan. We discussed what had happened, the impact on our congregations and what we might do as religious communities together. I can't recall anything specific coming from that meeting, though there was talk about things like interfaith prayer services. Later in the week I received a call from Victor Begg, a Muslim businessman who had been at the meeting. He gathered two other Muslims and three Christians who had all been vocal, calling for, in Victor's words, "doing more than praying and holding hands." Victor said that September 11th was the beginning of a new calendar, and we could not just do things the way we had in the past as religious communities living in polite isolation from each other apart from occasional interfaith dialogues and programs.

Six of us met on Victor's yacht moored at the Detroit Yacht Club. We talked and dreamed with intensity born out of the trauma of the terrorist attacks and the dreams of what might be if our faiths were focused on building peace in Detroit and perhaps even more distant parts of the world. We gathered a number of like-minded people from our networks for a series of meetings at a local hotel. Those early discussions included getting to know each other in more than superficial ways and envisioning what a vibrant inter-religious movement might look like that would help our community and contribute in some way to peace in the Middle East.

Then we realized that as Christians and Muslims we could not achieve what we wanted, especially if we ever hoped to impact the Middle East. We needed Jewish partners at the table, but if that partnership was to be genuine we couldn't just graft them in to what the Christians and Muslims had been doing for a year. The basic agreements for the group would have to be reworked and the trust would have to be established and built up to a level strong enough to handle the challenges we hoped to meet. So Jewish leaders were invited into our gatherings, and it seemed that we had to go right back to the beginning. The time was well spent, however, because in the end we had forged a partnership for interfaith work in Detroit that would prove strong enough to weather a number of challenges. We called ourselves Interfaith Partners.

As we looked for support for the interfaith actions we were envisioning, we were introduced to the Andrus Foundation, which works with community reconciliation projects using the transitions framework developed by William Bridges. Their assistance not only with funds but also with transitions training and collaboration in program design proved to be a huge boost to our young network.

During one of our gatherings Imam Abdul El-Amin, an African-American Muslim, told us that the book of Genesis tells about Ishmael and Isaac coming together to bury their father Abraham (see the story in Genesis 25.7-10). Abdul challenged us, "If Ishmael and Isaac could come together over their father Abraham, can't we today as Muslims, Jews and Christians come together over our common father Abraham?" That night, one of our Jewish partners, Brenda Rosenberg, had a dream about Isaac and Ishmael leaving the caves of Machpelah after burying their father together. As they started to turn away from each other, an Archangel Raphaela flew in from stage left and wrapped her wings around the grieving brothers. She then guided them through a four-step process of reconciliation: Breaking bread together, listening with compassion, stepping into the other's role, and then creating something new together. In Brenda's dream, the brothers agreed to write a play for teens on how compassionate listening can lead to understanding each other's positions and begin the reconciliation process. They also decided to include stories from teens that had undergone shifts in attitude to break the cycles of fear, hate and intolerance. Thus the Children of Abraham Project was conceived.

Acting upon her dream, Brenda brought together high school youth from Jewish, Muslim and Christian backgrounds for a three-month process of meeting together, eating lots of pizza, listening to each other's stories, role playing in which they stepped into the roles of youth from different traditions, and studying the ancient stories around Abraham. Rachel Urist, a professional playwright, and Rick Sperling, Director of the Mosaic Youth Theater, were brought into the group, and together a play was written. The play was based upon the story of Abraham along with Hagar and Ishmael and Sarah and Isaac. Around this ancient story in its various versions were woven the stories of youth in the Detroit area and the stories from the Middle East that connect to our Detroit communities. Youth acted in multiple roles in the energetic interplay of stories across time, geography and tradition. They also sang music drawn from all three faith traditions. Brenda recruited leaders of the three faiths to write portions of the script in which the clergy spoke about each religion's teaching on peace.

I accepted the challenge of writing the Christian part, putting into one minute of script a statement on peace that would be recognized by Orthodox, Catholic, Protestant and

Pentecostal Christians as their genuine expression on the topic. The completed draft of the play was read through by the youth before the Interfaith Partners, and the adults raised all sorts of issues. Intense discussions arose on topics such as Zionism and Christian evangelism and disagreements threatened to scuttle the whole project, but eventually solutions were found that pleased everyone. The youth in the project, meanwhile, were willing to go much further than the adults in risky discussions and built relationships among themselves.

When the first performance of "The Children of Abraham" was produced, it was a stunning success. A series of performances were held across the Detroit metro area. In most cases the performances were hosted by coalitions of local congregations from at least two different religions. Following the performances, small-group discussions were organized for people in the audience — or in some cases panels of men and women responded to audience questions from different faith communities. The cast traveled to other cities to put on the play, and CBS visited Detroit to do a program about "The Children of Abraham" and the interfaith movement that gave it birth.

Brenda saw a need to reach audiences across the United States and other countries. She spearheaded the development of a multi-media program called "Reuniting the Children of Abraham—a tool kit 4 peace." The program included portions of the play, interviews with the youthful participants and interviews with others in the Detroit interfaith community.

Educational material for the tool kit was developed with the University of Michigan on topics such as: frequently asked questions on Judaism, Christianity and Islam; how stereotyping can lead to violence; and "hot button" issues. Also included in the tool kit are guided meditations for peace, prayers for peace, and a step-by-step guide on how to bring the program to a community, school or religious institution. Brenda organized programs around the multi-media presentation that always incorporated direct interaction with people who came to view the program. The idea was not to entertain but to get people to talk to each other and begin the process of interfaith understanding, building relationships and building peace. Brenda has since presented "Reuniting the Children of Abraham" to more than 140 audiences, including presentations in Jerusalem and in Jordan with Arabic subtitles.

The Interfaith Partners made advocacy a key part of our joint actions. When the Islamic Center of America in Dearborn and the St. Mary's Assyrian Catholic Church in Warren were vandalized, partners from all the faith communities gathered to make a public witness against desecration of any house of

Interfaith Partners in solidarity at the Islamic Center of America after an act of vandalism

worship and against all forms of religious bigotry. When the President of Iran denigrated the Holocaust, the Interfaith Partners made a public statement at the Holocaust Memorial and toured it together. We realized that racial discrimination is closely tied to religious discrimination and is a common concern for all our religious traditions, so we joined in campaigns to combat racism and to educate people about the legacy of racism in our communities today. We also joined in a public witness at Central Michigan University after some students had hung nooses in a threatening racist prank. "Praying and holding hands" can be a powerful prophetic statement in pivotal places and times.

Our Interfaith Partners network was drawn from across the Detroit metropolitan area, but we were keenly aware that some local communities had their own interfaith groups. One group had grown up in the city of Troy following the refusal of Christians to allow Hindus to join in an annual National Day of Prayer.

The city of Hamtramck burst into national prominence when the broadcasting of the Muslim call to prayer became a political issue. The Al-Isla Mosque had approached the Hamtramck City Council about the matter, asking how the call to prayer might be amplified from the roof of the mosque in a way that would not unduly disrupt the neighborhood. The practice is common in countless Muslim neighborhoods around the world. The council reached unanimous agreement on reasonable hours for the practice. But some conservative Catholics developed a petition to put the matter on the ballot, and the call to prayer quickly became a heated political issue. A conservative Protestant group came up from Ohio to protest as national media attention began to focus on the controversy. But within Hamtramck itself, Catholic and Protestant leaders gathered with the leaders of the Muslim community to stand together for religious unity. Leaders from Interfaith Partners joined the fledgling Hamtramck interfaith group to provide guidance, encouragement and public support. At the election, the citizens of Hamtramck overwhelmingly supported the right of the mosque to broadcast the call to prayer.

The interfaith network that was born out of that controversy in Hamtramck continued to work together. They organized events for youth to visit different houses of worship including a synagogue in the nearby city of Oak Park. They hosted a "Children of Abraham" program and organized religiously diverse forums to discuss other important local issues with religious or moral dimensions.

Interfaith Partners continued to grow as an organization in significant ways. We expanded beyond the Abrahamic faiths, inviting Hindu and Sikh members onto our board. Our first expansion to welcome Jewish leaders had taken us back to foundational discussions and seemed to slow our progress, but this further addition of representatives from additional faiths moved ahead quickly. We realized that all of us had been changed by our interreligious interactions over the years in ways that expanded our thinking.

Our growth also was indicated in a profound way when we began holding spiritual retreats together. A retreat is a far different experience than a dialogue. Dialogues are head-to-head experiences that allow a good deal of personal distance from "the other" even as you discuss common matters. In a retreat, however, you are entering into a time and space of spiritual intimacy. A retreat is a heart-to-heart and spirit-to-spirit gathering. When the idea was first broached, the response was tepid. We were still too new to each other and didn't trust each other *that* much. The Andrus Foundation staff kept encouraging us to take that step, and finally the ripe moment came. We just knew we were ready, and the first of what has been five annual retreats (and counting) was held. Perhaps the most significant retreat in terms of symbolism was one focused on jazz as a metaphor for interfaith relationships. Detroit is a jazz city, so this metaphor spoke deeply to us, especially when the resource people were from a jazz combo that included a Baptist minister on guitar, a Muslim bassist and a Jewish drummer. The drummer couldn't make the retreat, but the other two combo members discussed their faith and the structure of jazz. Then they cut loose weaving their differences together to make incredible music. The interfaith jazz combo inspired us at so many levels and brought us together as a genuine community with our rich diversity of faith.

All was not sweetness and light, however. Just as violent actions far away drew us together, violent actions far away threatened to tear us apart. When the war erupted between Israel and Hezbollah, our Interfaith Partners group had close friends and colleagues in both Israel and Lebanon. Our neighbors were on both sides of the war, and the feelings were very intense. There were times when some of our members could barely speak to each other. In that tense setting some of the women from our network—Muslim, Jewish, Christian—joined together to form WISDOM, Women's Interfaith Solutions for Dialogue and Outreach in Metro Detroit (www.interfaithwisdom.org). WISDOM is now a non-profit organization with a diverse board of Muslim, Jewish, Christian, Bahá'í, Sikh, Hindu, Jain, and Buddhist women. The membership continues to expand as women from all walks of life join their mission and work together to make metropolitan Detroit a community of cultural and religious understanding through community service and educational programming. They visit each other's houses of worship to learn about each other's faith traditions. They also engage in projects such as Building Bridges with Habitat for Humanity, partnering with Kids Against Hunger, raising awareness about violence against women, and coming together for eco-friendly interfaith events at state parks. Some of the women have formed Peace X Peace groups linking to women's groups in places such as Indonesia and the Middle East (see Chapter 46 about Patricia Smith Melton, the founder of Peace X Peace). WISDOM has worked with other faith-based institutions in the community to sponsor interfaith dialogue, bring interfaith speakers to book fairs, set up interfaith panels at churches and synagogues, and visit photography exhibits, museums, and an interfaith labyrinth to spark educational interfaith exchange. WISDOM has made presentations for university seminars, diversity breakfasts, and cable TV programs to spread the word that people of diverse faiths, ethnicities and culture can come together in peace to expand their world views.

Gail Katz, one of the founders of WISDOM and a former English-as-a-Second-Language teacher, helped launch an educational project for middle school students called Religious Diversity Journeys. The program brought together 150 seventh graders drawn from six different schools to go on field trips to houses of worship and study Christianity, Judaism, Islam, Buddhism, Hinduism and Sikhism. The purpose of the Religious Diversity Journeys is to promote greater understanding, awareness and knowledge concerning the religions in our region and to prepare students for life in our increasingly diverse society. The teachers and students talked through issues of stereotyping, diversity and overcoming prejudice. Students learn about some of the traditions, culture and holidays associated with each faith, but are not preached to or proselytized. The program has grown as other school districts saw what was happening and wanted to participate. Other religions in the Detroit area are moving into the program, including Jainism and Native American religions. A congregational version of Religious Diversity Journeys is being developed to involve youth from local congregations of different faiths to share this religious exploration together, facilitated by Interfaith Partners staff.

Interfaith Partners is not an organization with hard boundary lines for membership and specific programs. It is a network with members and programs — but much more. With the support and under the umbrella of the Michigan Roundtable for Diversity and Inclusion (MRDI), Interfaith Partners has taken on some old interfaith programs, launched its own initiatives, and stimulated and spun off other initiatives. "Reuniting the Children of Abraham," WISDOM, Religious Diversity Journeys, and many other activities have developed out of the creative interaction of people who have come to know and trust each other. Sometimes programs are brought within the structure and staff of MRDI, and sometimes the programs operate separately under the leadership of the project visionary but with the support, publicity and recruitment of the other Interfaith Partners. This flexibility of structure and web of relationships has allowed for creativity and energy to be released and for ideas to find their best place to flourish. Many other projects have been developed that are not featured in this chapter, and the partners stimulate interfaith education and service in other institutions as they spread throughout the Detroit area.

As Victor Begg says, "September 11th started a new calendar." For some people that calendar is marked with fear. But for the current generation of interfaith heroes, the new calendar links people together as never before. New friendships are being made bridging religious communities. Interaction with people of other faiths is stimulating deeper engagement with the issues that challenge our communities. This is the situation in Detroit, but we are well aware that interfaith dynamism also is growing in many other communities across the United States as well as in other parts of the world.

The stories of interfaith heroes through history inspire us, but in this moment of world history — we are on stage. Each one of us. You, as you flip through the pages of this book.

Now is our time to act, and many people are choosing to act together, to learn from each other, and to build healthier, more just and more peaceful communities. We who have found this interfaith journey so invigorating invite others to plunge into the adventure.

Sources and Credits

Chapter 1: Interfaith Relationships

- "Tolerance Trio", Time.com archive from Feb. 11, 1935
- "Brother, Where Art Thou? The Origins and Development of the Interfaith Movement in America" by Joellyn Wallen Zollman, MyJewishLearning.com
- Archives, www.parliamentofreligions.org
- National Conference for Community and Justice, www.nccj.org
- The American Muslim, www.theamericanmuslim.org
- Official Website of A Common Word: www.acommonword.com
- Daniel Buttry, *Interfaith Heroes*, Read The Spirit Books
- Kevin Boyle, *Arc of Justice: A Saga of Race, Civil Rights, and Murder in the Jazz Age*, Owl Books

Chapter 2: Pope John Paul II

- The Vatican website: www.vatican.va
- *The Bible, The Jews and the Death of Jesus: A Collection of Catholic Documents*, Bishops' Committee for Ecumenical and Interreligious Affairs, United States Conference of Catholic Bishops
- Anti-Defamation League, *Pope John Paul II: An Appreciation: A Visionary Remembered*
- Israel News Agency: "Israel Mourns Death of Pope John Paul II" by Joel Leyden
- Photo: Public domain

Chapter 3: Baruch Tanembaum

- The International Raoul Wallenberg Foundation (www.raoulwallenberg.net)
- Honorable Tom Lantos of California, U.S. House of Representatives

- Photo: The International Raoul Wallenberg Foundation, used with permission

Chapter 4: Chiara Lubich

- BBC News, "Key Catholic Woman Activist Dies," March 14, 2008
- Focolare Website: www.rc.net/focolare
- Wikipedia

Chapter 5: Dalai Lama

- Official Website of the Dalai Lama: www.dalailama.com
- Nobel Prize Committee: www.nobelprize.org
- Photo: www.buddhismus.at/service/serv6.htm, used with permission
- Wikipedia

Chapter 6: Wayne Teasdale

- Wayne Teasdale's Interspirituality Website: http://home.comcast.net/~brotherwayne/index.htm
- What Is Englightenment? Magazine: www.wie.org
- Monastic Interreligous Dialogue: www.monasticdialog.com
- Wikipedia

Chapter 7: Ephraim Isaac

- *Peacemakers in Action: Profiles of Religion in Conflict Resolution*, edited by David Little, Tanenbaum Center for Interreligious Understanding, Cambridge University Press, 2007
- Institute on Religion and Public Policy: www.religionandpolicy.org/show.php?p=3.1.23
- "The Ethiopian Herald Interviews Professor Ephraim Isaac on the U.S. Ethiopian Diaspora," Ethiopian News Agency, *The Ethiopian Herald*, December 3, 2006
- Institute for Jewish and Community Research: www.jewishresearch.org
- Voice of America News: www.voanews.com

Chapter 8: Shanta Premawardhana

- National Council of Churches: www.ncccusa.org
- Religious Diversity News: www.pluralism.org
- Alliance of Baptists Newsletter, January 2008
- Fellowship of Reconciliation: www.interfaithfast.org
- Photo: http://www.ncccusa.org/news/03shanta.html

Chapter 9: David Rosen

- Rabbi David Rosen homepage: http://rabbidavidrosen.net
- American Jewish Committee: www.ajc.org
- "The First Alexandria Declaration of the Religious Leaders of the Holy Land," Alexandria, January 21, 2002, Israeli Ministry of Foreign Affairs
- "Middle East Conflict Threatens Global Peace" by Deidre May, Inter Press Service, August 28, 2006: www.commondreams.org
- Rabbis for Human Rights: http://rhr.israel.net/rabbis-for-human-rights
- E-mail interview between author and David Rosen, September 25, 2008
- Photo: Courtesy of David Rosen
- Wikipedia

Chapter 10: Interreligious Harmony

- Om-Guru, "A Short Biography of Ramakrishna Parmahamsa": http://www.om-guru.com/html/saints/ramakrishna.html
- Baha'i International Community: http://info.bahai.org/abdulbaha.html
- Vivekananda Vendanta Network: http://www.vivekananda.org
- Public Broadcasting Service: www.pbs.org/rootsinthesand/i_bhagat1.html
- "About Unity" www.unityonline.org

- BBW News, "Egyptian Film Laughs at Prejudice," http://news.bbc.co.uk/2/hi/middle_east/7525277.stm
- Daniel Buttry, *Interfaith Heroes*, Read The Spirit Books
- The Pluralism Project: http://www.pluralism.org/pluralism/what_is_pluralism.php
- Photo of Vivekananda: reproduced by permission of the Ramakrishna-Vivekananda Center of New York, USA; website: www.ramakrishna.org
- Photo of Adel Imam and Omar Sharif: http://news.bbc.co.uk/2/hi/middle_east/7525277.stm

Chapter 11: Sri Ramakrishna

- Ramakrishna-Vivekananda Center of New York: http://www.ramakrishna.org/
- Om-Guru, "A Short Biography of Ramakrishna Parmahamsa": http://www.om-guru.com/html/saints/ramakrishna.html
- Photograph reproduced by permission of the Ramakrishna-Vivekananda Center of New York, USA; Website: www.ramakrishna.org.
- Wikipedia

Chapter 12: Hazrat Inayat Khan

- Om-Guru, "A Short Biography of Hazrat Inayat Khan": http://www.om-guru.com/html/saints/khan.html
- Photo: http://www.om-guru.com/html/saints/khan.html (courtesy of Lightways)
- Or: http://dervish-healing-order.com/dhosem.htm
- Wikipedia, "Inayat Khan"

Chapter 13: Juliet Hollister

- Temple of Understanding: www.templeofunderstanding.org
- Saxon, Wolfgang, "Juliet Garretson Hollister, 84: Led Temple of Understanding," *New York Times*, November 30, 2000

- Photo: Courtesy of Temple of Understanding

Chapter 14: Hans Kung

- BeliefNet, www.beliefnet.com, "Towards a 'Continued Reformation of the Church': Interview with Hans Kung", Feb. 2004
- Hans Kung, "Explanatory Remarks Concerning a Declaration of the Religions for a Global Ethic", http://astro.temple.edu/~dialogue/Center/kung.htm
- "Declaration Toward a Global Ethic," Parliament of the World's Religions, 4 September 1993, Chicago. A downloadable copy can be found at: http://www.parliamentofreligions.org/_includes/FCKcontent/File/TowardsAGlobalEthic.pdf
- Photo: Manfred Grohe. © Stiftung Weltethos, used by permission
- Wikipedia

Chapter 15: Joseph H. Gelberman

- All-Faiths Seminary International website: www.allfaithseminary.org
- The New Seminary website: www.newseminary.org
- "A Quiet Interfaith Giant" by Rev. Jay Speights, Religion and Spirituality.com: www.religionandspirituality.com
- Photo: Courtesy of Joseph H. Gelberman, http://www.allfaithseminary.org/letter.asp

Chapter 16: Learning from Other Religions

- Ellsberg, Robert, *All Saints: Daily Reflections on Saints, Prophets, and Witnesses for Our Time*
- Image of Barlaam and Josaphat: Mackelvie Trust Collection, Auckland Art Gallery Toi o Tamaki, bequest of Dr Walter Auburn, 1982
- Image of Buddha: Courtesy of Anna Siudy, Prana Yogo Studio, www.pranayogastudio.com

Chapter 17: Zheng He

- "Admiral Zheng He," China Internet Information Center: http://www.china.org.cn/english/features/zhenhe/131897.htm
- David Kootnikoff, "Chinese Admiral's Legacy Ignites Tensions in Asia," OhmyNews
- http://english.ohmynews.com
- Jean Miyake Downey, "Ten Thousand Things," Kyoto Journal, www.kyotojournal.org
- Photo: http://www.time.com/time/asia/features/journey2001/intro.html (Zheng He Institute) (or http://zhenghe.webs.com/apps/photos/photo.jsp?photoID=75102&prev=1)
- Wikipedia

Chapter 18: Kabir

- "Kabir: Mystic Philosopher," Colorado State University: www.cs.colostate.edu/~malaiya/kabir.html
- Poetry Chaikhana: Sacred Poetry from Around the World: www.poetry-chaikhana.com/K/Kabir
- Rajender Krishan, Boloji.com: www.boloji.com/kabir
- *Songs of Kabir*, translated by Rabindranath Tagore, assisted by Evelyn Underhill
- Wikipedia
- Poet Seers: http://www.poetseers.org/the_poetseers/kabir/
- Picture: www.saranaagathi.files.wordpress.com, used by permission

Chapter 19: Evelyn Underhill

- The Evelyn Underhill Association, http://www.evelynunderhill.org/
- Dana Greene, "Adhering to God: The Message of Evelyn Underhill for Our Times," *Spirituality Today*, Spring 1987
- Aramcha: The Cloud of Unknowing, http://anamchara.com/mystics/evelyn-underhill/

- Susie Sheldrake, "Life of Evelyn Under: An Intimate Portrait of the Groundbreaking Author of Mysticism/ Evelyn Underhill: Essential Writings, The" book reviews published in Anglican Theological Review, Spring, 2004
- *Songs of Kabir*, translated by Rabindranath Tagore, assisted by Evelyn Underhill
- Photo: http://www.evelynunderhill.org/
- Wikipedia

Chapter 20: Simone Weil

- The Simone Weil Homepage: http://members.aol.com/geojade/
- About Simone Weil: http://simoneweil.net/home.htm
- Joy Palmer, "Simone Weil" in *Fifty Key Educational Thinkers*, Routledge, 2001
- Wikipedia

Chapter 21: Mohandas Gandhi, Martin Luther King, Jr. and Aung San Suu Kyi

- *A Testament of Hope: The Essential Writings and Speech of Martin Luther King, Jr.*, edited by James M. Washington, Harper, 1986
- Aung San Suu Kyi, *Freedom from Fear and Other Writings*, Viking Press, 1991
- James D. Hunt, "Adin Ballou, Tolstoy and Gandhi," http://www.adinballou.org/BallouTolstoyGandhi.shtml
- "Aung San Suu Kyi – Biography," http://nobelprize.org
- Mahatma Gandhi, *The Story of My Experiments with Truth*
- *A Testament of Hope: The Essential Writings and Speeches of Martin Luther King, Jr.*, edited by James M. Washington, Harper Collins
- Photo of Aung San Suu Kyi: Public domain
- Photos of Mahatma Gandhi and Martin Luther King, Jr.: public domain

Chapter 22: E. Stanley Jones

- United Christian Ashrams: "E. Stanley Jones: Missionary Extraordinaire," http://vaxxine.com/eves/jones.htm
- William Berg, "My 30 Years with E. Stanley Jones," in *Show Me the Way to Go Home.* http://bergbooks.com/jones.htm
- Photo: Public Domain
- Wikipedia

Chapter 23: Thomas Merton

- The Thomas Merton Center: http://www.mertoncenter.org/
- Alan Altany, "What was the Christian monk looking to find in his dialogue with Buddhism?" from The Thomas Merton Collection: www.hundredmountain.com
- Jim Knight, "The Thomas Merton We Knew": www.therealmerton.com
- William Apel, *Signs of Peace: The Interfaith Letters of Thomas Merton*, Orbis Books
- Photo: The Thomas Merton Center
- Wikipedia

Chapter 24: Karen Armstrong and Bruce Feiler

- Photos: Armstrong: by Jerry Bauer
- and Feiler: www.brucefeiler.com/images/bruce_about.jpg
- Ethan Zuckerman blog: http://www.ethanzuckerman.com/blog/
- *Mary Rourke meets the author of "Islam, a short history"*, Los Angeles Times, October 9, 2000
- Jane Lampman, "After falling away, she fell in love with religion again," *The Christian Science Monitor*, March 30, 2004: http://www.csmonitor.com/2004/0330/p16s01-bogn.htm
- Westar Institute: www.westarinstitute.org

- Book Browse: http://www.bookbrowse.com/author_interviews/full/index.cfm?author_number=813
- Bruce Feiler: www.brucefeiler.com
- Wikipedia

Chapter 25: Religious Liberty

- Daniel Buttry, *Interfaith Heroes,* Read The Spirit Books
- Rev. Protopresbyter George C. Papademetriou, *An Orthodox Christian View of Non-Christian Religions,* Greek Orthodox Archdiocese of America: http://www.goarch.org/en/ourfaith/articles/article8089.asp
- R. Gustav Neibuhr, "On Faith," Newsweek Online: http://newsweek.washingtonpost.com/onfaith/r_gustav_niebuhr/
- Margaret Bacon, "Let Me Be the One: Mary Dyer, Witness to Religious Liberty," *The Universe Bends Toward Justice,* New Society Publishers
- Wikipedia
- Photo of Cyrus Cylinder: from Livius.Org, with permission
- Photo of Roger Williams statue: Public domain
- Photo of Mary Dyer statue: Public domain

Chapter 26: Ashoka

- *The Edicts of King Ashoka,* an English rendering by Ven. S. Dhammika, Buddhist Publication Society, http://www.cs.colostate.edu/~malaiya/ashoka.html
- "Ashoka the Great" www.4to40.com
- Michael Hart, *The 100: A Ranking of the Most Influential Persons in History,* Citadel Press
- Wikipedia
- Picture of Ashoka: Public Domain

Chapter 27: Abd ar-Rahman III and Al-Hakam II

- Encyclopedia of World Biography, www.bookrags.com

- "Hakam II, Al-," *The Columbia Encyclopedia*, Sixth Edition, 2004, Columbia University Press.
- Nofal Ahmad Al-Abdulali: http://www.idir.net/~suede/successor1.html
- Wikipedia
- Picture of Add-ar-Rahman III: Public domain

Chapter 28: John Sigismund and Isabella Jagiello

- David Parke, *The Epic of Unitarianism*: http://webuus.com/timeline/Sigismund_Toleration.html
- Kay Saucier, "A Unitarian King and a Unitarian Prophet": www.uufhc.net/s040815.html
- Alison Wohler, "Historically Speaking: An Intergenerational Service": http://www.uusocietyamherst.org/documents/HistoricallySpeaking.pdf
- Wikipedia
- Picture of Isabella Jagiello: Public domain
- Picture of John Sigismund: Public domain

Chapter 29: Haym Salomon

- Jewish World Review: http://www.jewishworldreview.com/jewish/salomon.asp
- National Park Service: http://www.nps.gov/revwar/about_the_revolution/haym_salomom.html
- Jewish Virtual Library: http://www.jewishvirtuallibrary.org/jsource/biography/salomon.html
- Address by Alan D. Corré, University of Wisconsin at Milwaukee: http://www.uwm.edu/~corre/occasionala/salomon.html
- Wikipedia
- Picture of Haym Salomon: Public domain
- Stamp: Courtesy of U.S. Postal Service

Chapter 30: John Leland

- Charles Hyneman and Donald Lutz, *Political Writing During the Founding Era: 1760-1805*: http://candst.tripod.com/tnppage/qleland.htm
- The Reformed Reader: http://www.reformedreader.org/leland.htm
- William Cathcart, *Baptist Encyclopedia*, "John Leland"
- Wikipedia
- Picture of John Leland: Public domain

Chapter 31: Providing Refuge

- Ma'sood Cajee, "Between European hypocrisy and Iranian folly: The cartoon controversy, the Holocaust, and the legacy of Nuremburg," Fellowship of Reconciliation: www.forusa.org/articlesandresources/hypocrisyandfolly.html
- New Sanctuary Movement: www.newsanctuarymovement.org
- Tania Leah Haas and Sarah Brown, "Sanctuary: Old Idea, New Movement," News 21:
- http://news21project.org/story/2007/07/27/sanctuary_old_idea_new_movement
- Alexia Salvatierra, "Sacred Refuge" *Sojourners Magazine*, September/October 2007
- Charles Weinblatt's webblog: http://cweinblatt.wordpress.com/2008/09/01/the-meaning-of-life/
- Peter Hellman, *When Courage Was Stronger Than Fear: Remarkable Stories of Christians and Muslims Who Saved Jews from the Holocaust*, MJF Books

Chapter 32: Irena Sendler

- Life in a Jar: The Irena Sendler Project: www.irenasendler.org
- Louis Bülow, "The Holocaust: Crimes, Heroes and Villain": www.auschwitz.dk/Sendler.htm
- Wikipedia

- Photo: Life in a Jar: The Irena Sendler Project, used by permission

Chapter 33: Titus Brandsma

- Ellsberg, Robert, *All Saints: Daily Reflections on Saints, Prophets, and Witnesses for Our Time*
- Carmelite Net: http://carmelnet.org/titus/titus.htm
- Boniface Hanley, O.F.M., "No Strangers to Violence, No Strangers to Love," published by Ave Maria Press
- Photo and stained glass image: Courtesy of Carmelite Press and Carmelite Net

Chapter 34: Si Kaddour ben Ghabrit

- *Islam en France 1830-1962*: http://islamenfrance.canalblog.com/archives/2007/02/10/4057434.html
- "Kabyls who helped save Jews from the Nazis," Kabylia Observer: www.kabylia.info/observer/spip.php?article33
- Ma'sood Cajee, "Between European hypocrisy and Iranian folly: The cartoon controversy, the Holocaust, and the legacy of Nuremburg," Fellowship of Reconciliation: www.forusa.org/articlesandresources/hypocrisyandfolly.html
- Ma'sood Cajee, "On Holocaust Zeroes and Heroes," Altmuslim: www.altmuslim.com
- Bureau of International Information Programs, U.S. Department of State, "Scholar Discusses Arab, Muslim Aid to Jews During Holocaust": http://usinfo.state.gov/usinfo/Archive/2007/Apr/10-760308.html
- Photo: http://islamenfrance.canalblog.com/

Chapter 35: Dervis Korkut

- Peter Hellman, *When Courage Was Stronger Than Fear: Remarkable Stories of Christians and Muslims Who Saved Jews from the Holocaust*, MJF Books
- Ma'sood Cajee, "Between European hypocrisy and Iranian folly: The cartoon controversy, the Holocaust,

and the legacy of Nuremburg," Fellowship of Reconciliation: www.forusa.org/articlesandresources/hypocrisyandfolly.html
- Ma'sood Cajee, "On Holocaust Zeroes and Heroes," Altmuslim: www.altmuslim.com
- Pierre Tristam, Candide's Notebooks: http://www.pierretristam.com/Bobst/07/cn120607.htm
- Wikipedia
- Picture of Sarajevo Haggadah: http://www.pierretristam.com/Bobst/07/cn120607.htm

Chapter 36: Corrie Ten Boom

- The Corrie Ten Boom Museum: http://www.corrietenboom.com/
- Wheaton College Archives: http://www.wheaton.edu/bgc/archives/GUIDES/078.htm#3
- Corrie Ten Boom, *The Hiding Place*, Chosen Books
- Wikipedia
- Photo: http://en.wikipedia.org/wiki/Image:Corrie_ten_Boom.jpg#filehistory

Chapter 37: Building Just and Peaceful Communities

- "Isaiah Wall" Photo: Public Domain
- Photo of World Conference of Religions for Peace, courtesy of Religions for Peace
- International Fellowship of Reconciliation: www.ifor.org
- World Conference of Religions for Peace: www.wcrp.org

Chapter 38: Charles Andrews

- NationMaster Encyclopedia: http://www.nationmaster.com/encyclopedia/Charles-F.-Andrews
- Photo: Copyright: Isa Sarid/GandhiServe, used with permission—all other rights reserved
- Wikipedia

Chapter 39: Dorothy Day

- Jim Forest: "A Biography of Dorothy Day," The Catholic Worker: http://www.catholicworker.org/Dorothyday/
- Beth Randall, "Illuminating Lives: Dorothy Day": http://www.cs.drexel.edu/~gbrandal/Illum_html/Day.html
- Le Anne Schreiber, review of *Breaking Bread: The Catholic Worker and the Origin of Catholic Radicalism in America* by Mel Piehl, *New York Times*, December 22, 1982
- Wikipedia
- Photo: Courtesy of the Marquette University Archives

Chapter 40: Stephen Wise

- Jewish Virtual Library: http://www.jewishvirtuallibrary.org/jsource/biography/wise.html
- Harvard Square Library, "Stephen Wise": http://www.harvardsquarelibrary.org/reverend/05wise.htm
- Seymour "Sy" Brody, "Rabbi Stephen Wise: A Leader in Zionism and Social Reform" *Jewish Heroes and Heroines of America*, Lifetime Books
- Wikipedia
- Photo: Library of Congress

Chapter 41: Masahisa Goi

- Byakko Shinko Kai: http://www.byakko.org/1_about/goi/index.html
- World Peace Prayer Society: http://www.worldpeace.org/wpps.html
- Photo: http://www.byakko.org/1_about/goi/index.html
- Peace Pole Image: Courtesy of Peace Pole Makers: www.peacepoles.com

Chapter 42: Richard St. Barbe Baker

- Men of the Trees: http://www.menofthetrees.com.au/history.html
- Saskatchewan's Environmental Champions: http://www.econet.sk.ca/sk_enviro_champions/richard_baker.html
- Edward Goldsmith, "Richard St. Barbe Baker: A Tribute": http://www.edwardgoldsmith.org/page124.html
- Wikipedia
- Photo: http://www.econet.sk.ca/sk_enviro_champions/richard_baker.html

Chapter 43: Thich Nhat Hanh

- Plum Village Practice Center: http://www.plumvillage.org/HTML/ourteacher.html
- Michael and Sharee Cox: http://www.seaox.com/thich.html
- Dharma Memphis: http://www.dharmamemphis.com/magnolia/tnhbio.html
- *A Testament of Hope: The Essential Writings and Speeches of Martin Luther King, Jr.*, edited by James M. Washington, Harper Collins
- Wikipedia

hapter 44: Karim al-Hussayni, Aga Khan IV

- Aga Khan Development Network: http://www.akdn.org/
- International Baccalaureate Organization: http://www.ibo.org/
- Associated Press, "Aga Khan to tour US to mark his 50th anniversary as the imam for Ismaili Muslims," April 11, 2008
- South Asian Media, "Prince Karim Aga visits BD," May 20, 2008
- Global Atlanta, "Muslim Spiritual Leader Helps International Baccalaureate Celebrate 40th Anniversary"

- by Trevor Williams, April 24, 2008: http://stories.globalatlanta.com/2008stories/016120.html
- Wikipedia
- Photo: Public Domain

Chapter 45: Sulak Sivaraksa

- Sathirakoses-Nagapradipa Foundation: www.sulak-sivaraksa.org
- Right Livelihood Award: http://www.rightlivelihood.org/sulak.html
- Sulak Sivaraksa homepage: http://sivaraksa.com/biography/
- Photo: Courtesy of Sulak Sivaraksa and *Seeds of Peace*, Bangkok, Thailand
- Wikipedia

Chapter 46: Patricia Smith Melton

- PeaceXPeace: http://www.peacexpeace.org/content/
- The Melton Foundation: www.meltonfoundation.org
- Photo from The Melton Foundation
- "Meet Patricia Smith Melton of Peace X Peace," WE Magazine for Women: http://wemagazineforwomen.com/meet-patricia-smith-welton-of-peace-x-peace/
- Molly Mayfield Barbee, Interfaith Heroes nomination: www.ReadTheSpirit.com
- Photo: http://www.meltonfoundation.org/mainsite/founders.htm

Chapter 47: Gaston Grandjean Dayanand

- City of Joy Aid: www.cityofjoyaid.org/bio_grandjean.html
- Southern Health Improvement Samity, http://www.shisindia.org/gaston.html
- Sreemanti Ghosh, "The Craftsman of Hope," Express India: http://cities.expressindia.com/fullstory.php?newsid=226125

- Gaston Dayanand website, Bengali Chronicles: http://www.gaston-dayanand.com/e/gaston-dayanand.asp
- Photo: http://www.gaston-dayanand.com/e/bengali-chronicles%20.asp

Chapter 48: A.T. Ariyaratne

- Sarvodaya USA: http://www.sarvodayausa.org/founder.php
- *Newsweek*, "A Conscientious Objector": http://www.newsweek.com/id/118140
- A.T. Ariyaratne, "A Wake Up Call," Yes Magazine: http://www.yesmagazine.org/article.asp?ID=509
- A.T. Ariyaratne, "Application of Gandhian and Buddhist Principles of Non-Violence to Combat Fanaticism," Nuremberg Forum, Sept. 2000: http://www.evrel.ewf.uni-erlangen.de/pesc/R2000-Ariyaratne.htm
- Wikipedia
- Photo: Courtesy of Sarvodaya USA

Chapter 49: James Wuye and Muhammed Ashafa

- James Movel Wuye and Muhammed Nurayn Ashafa, *The Pastor and the Imam: Responding to Conflict*
- World Learning: http://www.worldlearning.org/6568.htm
- Tanenbaum Center for Interreligious Understanding, *Peacemakers in Action: Profiles of Religion in Conflict Resolution*
- Eliza Grizwald, "God's Country," *The Atlantic*, March, 2008
- Michael Henderson, "The Imam and The Pastor", http://www.stethelburgas.org/documents/theimamandthepastor.pdf
- Photo: Courtesy of CONTACT program: www.sit.edu/contact

Chapter 50: It's Our Turn Now

- Michigan Roundtable for Diversity and Inclusion: http://www.miroundtable.org/mrdi/
- Poster: Courtesy of Rediscovering the Children of Abraham
  Photo: Courtesy of Michigan Roundtable for Diversity and Inclusion

Sources and Credits

About the Author

Daniel L. Buttry is the Global Consultant for Peace and Justice for International Ministries of the American Baptists Churches (ABC). In that capacity he works around the world doing training in conflict transformation, nonviolence and peacebuilding. He has been part of mediation teams in relation to conflicts in Burma (Myanmar) and with the Nagas of Northeast India. He is the author of a number of books, most notably *Christian Peacemaking: From Heritage to Hope* and . He has pastored churches in Boston and Detroit, directed the Peace Program for the ABC, and represented the ABC at the United Nations as a Non-Governmental Organizations delegate. He is a founding member of Interfaith Partners in Detroit. His wife Sharon is an ordained American Baptist clergyperson, and they have three adult children. They live in Hamtramck, Michigan.

Colophon

This book was produced using methods that separate content from presentation. Doing so increases the flexibility and accessibility of the content and allows us to generate editions in different presentation formats quickly and easily.

The content is stored in a standard XML format called DocBook 5 (www.DocBook.org). Adobe InDesign®, the Oxygen® XML Editor and Microsoft Word® were used in the production.

- The print edition is set in Adobe Arno Pro type.
- Cover art and design by Rick Nease (www.RickNease.com).
- Editing by David Crumm.
- Digital encoding and print layout by John Hile.

CPSIA information can be obtained at www.ICGtesting.com
Printed in the USA
BVOW011700050313

314714BV00008B/126/P

9 781934 879146